UNNECESSARY COMPLICATIONS

Christian Dating in
a Modern World

DAVID MILLS

Ordering Information:

Available at www.unnecessarycomplications.com

ISBN: 978-1-7324094-0-8

ePub ISBN: 978-1-7324094-1-5

Library of Congress Control Number: 2018906408

Printed in the United States of America

First Edition

14 13 12 11 10 / 10 9 8 7 6 5 4 3 2 1

Table of Contents

To The Chapel youth ministry. Sorry this took me so long, guys.

Introduction

"He who finds a wife finds a good thing and obtains favor from the Lord."

—Proverbs 18:22

I DON'T KNOW if getting married will ever be easy for anyone by any stretch of the imagination, but the whole process of finding a spouse doesn't have to be as hard as we have made it, especially for people who are Christians. I wrote this book to help parse out a talk I gave about how to approach dating in a way that more closely aligns with the relationship structures God sets up for us in the Bible. Once you understand how God structures relationships, you can better understand how all of your relationships are supposed to align with each other and things start to work together for good.

The way that society currently dates is, at best, unhelpful to your future marriage and, at worst, harmful to your future marriage. Besides the fact that society's way of dating makes it harder for people to find a mate in the first place, the baggage and bad habits people can so easily pick up along the way create unnecessary complications in relationships once people finally do get married. I want to talk about why this is and how to prevent avoidable conflict in marriage that is born in dating. The unavoidable problems are bad enough on their own; they don't need company. If you are going to get married, you will have to walk from point A of singleness, to point B of marriage, but you don't have to walk uphill and carry unnecessary weight into your life together.

So many Christians seem to date in a way that is very similar to the way the rest of the world dates, only they throw a cross around its neck. Other Christians try to avoid all the pitfalls and mistakes that the world ends up unwittingly jumping into by calling dating "courting" or by trying to avoid dating altogether. For the most part when I talk about dating, I'm including "courting" as well. I think that both methods have their advantages and disadvantages and you will see elements of both in what I suggest, but I believe they both miss the mark. The problem is our dating paradigm. We let society set the parameters of the area between singleness and marriage and then we try to figure out how to live out our Christianity as best as possible within that paradigm, as if stuck in immovable constraints. I believe there is a better way and the world's constraints are not immovable. We need to change our relationship paradigm.

God really does give relationship guidance if you're ready to hear it.

I grew up hearing that God doesn't really talk about dating in the Bible. This is a true statement – unless you count Ruth and Boaz on the threshing floor.[1] Along with this, I grew up hearing well-meaning Christians start making stuff up with the best of intentions, many times using the Bible as much as they could to guide young people (and not so young people) who found themselves in the season of life where they were searching for a mate. Some people

---

1 Which let's be honest, no one ever does, nor should they.

would get really good results from the made-up advice of others, and other people not so much. Some made-up advice is always going to be better than other made-up advice. The interesting and crucial part of all the advice given becomes: in what way or to what extent is the advice you are getting tied to God's Word?

Enter Joshua Harris. *I Kissed Dating Goodbye*[2] was the first Christian dating book I'd ever heard of. I bet it was the first Christian dating book most people thought existed until they read it and saw that he referenced Elisabeth Elliot's *Passion and Purity*[3] . And for those of us who didn't even read *I Kissed Dating Goodbye*, his book became a very convenient punching bag and punchline in Christian circles. Over the years, I came across many other Christian dating books that were a lot worse than *I Kissed Dating Goodbye*. I only came across a few that were better. Apparently, Christian dating books are not easy to write.

In the course of my life volunteering and working in youth ministry, and college ministry, I was exposed to many, many books on dating. Some of them were written for secular audiences. Most were for Christian audiences and many of them had some redeeming qualities. In fact, I reference several of them in here. In a field with so many books, we need more of them to be good. This is my attempt to write another good one.

A couple of years before I wrote this book, I started telling people about my ideas. People couldn't argue against what I said using the Bible; I suspect that's because what I had to say were the most biblically aligned ideas about dating that I (and likely they as well) had ever heard. The most compelling argument against what I said came from my friend, Anna, who said, "I agree with

---

2 Harris, Joshua (1997). *I Kissed Dating Goodbye*, Multnomah Books.
3 Elliot, Elisabeth (1984). *Passion and Purity*, Baker Book House.

everything you said, except for the general impossibility of all of it." This is my attempt to explain the impossible.

What I write in this book is very different from the way that almost everyone goes about dating. I do need to say, in the old way of doing things, finding a mate in a God-honoring way is not impossible. It's just so much harder, and unnecessarily so. This new way is not going to eliminate all of the problems. It will just make most of the problems so much more easily recognizable and avoidable. This levels the playing field instead of making Christians climb uphill. Instead of taking the dating formula from culture and throwing a cross around its neck, we need to start with God's Word and go from there. As a result, the way we operate in our male/female relationships will not only honor God by our behaviors, but more importantly reflect His intent and design for sex and relationships to a watching world.

I hope you read this. I hope it makes sense. I hope it helps.

The Desire for Marriage

"I don't ever want to get married."

—My sister

That was one of the last things I heard before I decided I had to write this book.

This is not a book about marriage. But I have to start with marriage because without marriage, dating is pointless.

Some people are called to be single.

The premise of this book is aimed directly at people who want to be married someday and the point of this chapter is to talk about why marriage is good and desirable. I believe one of the many reasons God created marriage is because it is a good thing He wants us to enjoy. I need to be clear, though: just because marriage is good does not mean that singleness is bad.

If you become an adult and you never want to get married, it does not mean there is anything wrong with you or your desires. Not wanting to get married, either in the short term or indefinitely, is not an indication that there is anything wrong with you.

People will sometimes make statements like, "You are so great; I don't understand why you are still single." These statements, however well-meaning they are, generally seem to be accompanied by the implication that there is something wrong with not being married, or even worse, that there is something wrong with *you* because you are not married. This is not the case.

Being unmarried without the desire to be married can be a very good thing. The Apostle Paul tells us in a letter he wrote to the ancient church of Corinth, "To the unmarried and the widows I say that it is good for them to remain single, as I am. But if they cannot exercise self-control, they should marry. For it is better to marry than to burn with passion."[4] God's Word says that it is good to remain single. He says if you are not married and you have enough self-control to control your sexual desires, stay unmarried. So many people take it as a given that people are supposed to get married, that people are naturally going to want to get married. This is not necessarily the case. If you are reading this and you don't have a particular temptation towards sexual immorality[5] because you have enough self-control, stay single!

Take advantage of the fact that you are single and can remain so. Your ability to serve others and the variety of service you can offer is almost always much greater when you are not married. The quality of life you get to live is not necessarily any better or worse when single as opposed to being married. It is different if you are married, but different can be good or bad on both sides. In fact, depending on who you are, different can be awful. There is only one realm of existence where getting married is definitively better: if you don't have self-control sexually, it is better to be married.

---

4 1 Corinthians 7:8-9

5 We will talk more about sexual immorality later; also, the way Paul talks about sexuality in relation to marriage in this chapter seems to completely validate the way we will talk about sexuality in relation to dating.

Other than that, singleness is such a good thing. Don't waste your singleness trying to get out of being single if you don't have to.

Relatedly, being unmarried with the desire to be married can be a very good thing. If you know you have the desire to be married, the single state is still the superior state for spiritual things such as ministry and service, and also for more secular things such as career advancement and self-improvement. All else being equal, you can get a lot more done in most realms of life when you are unmarried. You will never have so much time to grow and improve as a person as when you are single.

Bridling sexuality is definitely more difficult when you are not married, but everything else brings advantages to remaining unmarried. There are many, many more accessible books, articles, and other resources geared towards taking the desire to be married into marriage than there are maximizing singleness while single, even with a desire to be married. Please do not make the mistake of thinking that because the people who care about you (and even the people who don't so much) seem to expect you to get married, being married is better than being single. Being married is good, but it's not better.

But what about God saying, "It is not good that the man should be alone"[6]? There is that. And to that I would say, it is not good for man to be alone. God got that one right.[7] But there are more ways to be not alone than married. At the point when God made that statement, there was exactly one human being on earth and it was not good for that man to be alone. When it comes to humanity, it is impossible for man to be more alone than if there are literally zero other people. And yes, the second person was his wife and with his wife he was no longer alone; but being

---

6 Genesis 2:18

7 And every other one as well.

unmarried and being alone are not the same thing. Being unmarried and being alone are not even synonyms for one another. God says, "It is not good that the man should be alone." He does not say, "It is not good for man to be unmarried" because that is not true. We don't have to be married to the people we're around in order for it to count as not being alone.

I feel the need to say it clearly: being single does not make you "less than." Being unmarried does not make you "not good." There is a difference between being unmarried and being alone. Some people are definitely designed[8] to remain unmarried. It's just not most of us.

Just because you haven't seen a good one does not mean they don't exist.

The first marriage of 34.7% of all women ended in annulment, separation or divorce.[9] Depending on who you talk to or what you read, that statistic can be much higher. It seems like the statistic American culture has grabbed onto most goes like this, "50% of all marriages end in divorce." This statistic is more or less true.[10] The bottom line is our society has a negative view of marriage. It seems like most of the marriages people ever witness are hard or unhappy or downright ugly.

> "I think I might never go to men again. I think I won't ever do the whole men thing anymore or get married. I'm just done with men."

---

8 Some people might say "called" but I'm not saying that because I've never known what that really means.

9 *Centers for Disease Control and Prevention. "D Listing, Key Statistics from the National Survey of Family Growth".*

10 I don't have an original source for this stat, but the sentiment is what matters most in this sentence.

"You're saying you don't want to be with anyone, ever, for the rest of your life."

"I mean, I may French kiss someone."

"Of course."

"I might French kiss someone, but I'm not going to marry anyone." [11]

When Britney Spears recorded the above segment on *The Late, Late Show with James Corden* in 2016, she was already the mother of two, had been married twice, and divorced twice. Two years before Britney's first marriage, her own parents got divorced.[12] It's easy to understand that if anyone else had had the experiences Britney had and knew what she knew, they would feel the same way and think the same things. Without knowing her personally, it's easy to glean that her most personal experiences with marriage have not been positive, so of course she is not going to want to go through something like that again.

Albert Einstein's definition of insanity is doing the same thing over and over again but expecting different results.[13] If all your experiences with marriage are bad, it seems like you would have to be insane to want to get married. If all you know of the results of marriage is pain and heartache, why would you (assuming you are rational) want to intentionally subject yourself to such pain and heartache?

11 Britney Spears Carpool Karaoke – *The Late Late Show with James Corden*. https://www.youtube.com/user/TheLateLateShow

12 Lynne Spears «*Britney's Next Act*». *People.* September 2, 2002. *"Report: Britney Spears' parents reconciling"*

13 Nobody really knows for certain if Albert Einstein originated this quote, but it could have been him.

Marriage is more than a wedding.

Weddings in America are a big deal. The wedding industry in the United States is big business.[14] If you've ever been asked to be a part of a bridal party and had to buy a dress or rent a tuxedo, you have been given the smallest glimpse into how expensive the whole ordeal can be. The average cost of a wedding in the United States is $26,645.[15] Weddings in our culture are built up by seemingly everyone. Brides are told their wedding day is one of the most important days of their lives. Conversely, brides are also told that their wedding day is *not* one of the most important days of their lives. Any day that gets the billing from both sides of the coin is obviously a big deal.

Weddings signify something new. They represent two people coming together to form something that is bigger than those two individuals. Wedding days are days when family and friends can come together and celebrate people they love.

It's impossible to say empirically, but it seems like personal impulse and society both put more of an emphasis on preparing for the wedding than the marriage. Wedding festivities in the United States usually last no longer than a few days. Almost always, a marriage is going to last longer than that.

For better or worse, it seems like our society is very much for weddings and very much against marriage. This contradiction is remedied by divorce. Divorce lets people have the wedding of their dreams, but at the same time escape from the nightmare of marriage. The problem is, this way of doing things is robbing people of the very things they want most.[16]

---

14 IBIS World, Wedding Industry. *http://www.ibisworld.com/industry/default. aspx?indid=2008*

15 Cost of Wedding.com. *http://www.costofwedding.com/*

16 And robbing God of what He wants most: His glory.

Ecclesiastes 4:9-12

Solomon, the wisest man to ever live, seemed to think being alone is not something one should desire on principle. He says, "Two are better than one, because they have a good reward for their toil. For if they fall, one will lift up his fellow. But woe to him who is alone when he falls and has not another to lift him up! Again, if two lie together, they keep warm, but how can one keep warm alone? And though a man might prevail against one who is alone, two will withstand him – a threefold cord is not quickly broken."[17]

Now is as good a time as any to reiterate that you don't have to be married to avoid being alone. In fact, these verses are true and should apply to your life whether you are married or not. If you are going through life alone, it will be harder for you, if not impossible. If you do stumble, having another person there to lift you up is an unadulterated blessing! People who are in a Christ-centered marriage have that person to encourage them, to lift them up when they need lifting, to support and nurture and edify. A person in a healthy, Christ-centered marriage can live all of life with greater impact in any given situation. If you were to approach a task with a friend or a partner as an unmarried person, imagine approaching that same task with that same friend or partner AND your spouse! A threefold cord is not quickly broken! I would never recommend someone get married solely for the sake of efficiency in life, but if you like the idea of efficiency, perhaps marriage is for you.

Life is easier with a partner.

A little while ago I was saying that life is not better for a person simply because he or she is married. This is true, but life can definitely be easier with a partner. Now I should say it upfront, if you

---

17 Ecclesiastes 4:9-12

are married to someone but you aren't operating as partners, then this is a recipe for a major disaster and your life will not be easier. The mere fact of being married to someone does not mean that you are partners. It should mean that, and it is a sin and a shame when marriage does not mean that, but those two things are not the same. In fact, if you grew up in a home where your parents ended up getting divorced, you probably witnessed the lack of a partnership first-hand.

When a marriage is one of a partnership, life is easier. It will be easier for you financially. It will be easier to spend and save money well, whether you have one or two incomes. It will be easier to exist in social settings. Especially if one of you is introverted, having a partner will make the social situations better; and even if both of you love being the life of the party – if you are acting as partners, and not competing for attention, thriving in those settings will be even easier.

Having a partner to whom you are married comes with all sorts of advantages. You will be less likely to forget things because there will be someone else to remind you or remember for you. You will be able to accomplish more things at once because you have the ability to split up and focus on different tasks if you need to. One of you will likely be taller than the other, so you both get the advantages of height. You get to think about confusing problems in different ways. And this one cannot be understated: you will have someone to tell you when you're being dumb. You need this because sometimes you don't know. But she knows. And she will tell you.[18] Say thank you.

---

18 When you are married, and you are telling your spouse that he or she is being dumb, you always need to do it with grace and truth; do not forget grace.

Sanctification

If you care about sanctification (growing more in the likeness of Jesus Christ), marriage is the thing for you. Marriage counselor Steven Fox says that being single gives you the greatest opportunity to grow in ministry, but being married gives you the greatest opportunity to grow in holiness.[19] There is absolutely no limit to the amount of ministry one can do whether they are single or married, and there is absolutely no limit to the amount of sanctification that can take place in your life whether you are single or married, but it is undeniable that circumstances play into the way you will grow.

You can become an expert downhill skier and live in Florida 11 months out of the year, but if you live in Switzerland 12 months out of the year with the same desire to become an expert, you will be much more likely to succeed if you are around snow most of the time. When you live so closely with another person who can always see all your sin, you will have more opportunity and motivation to deal with that sin. Getting married gives you a greater chance to see your selfishness and pride and all the other sins that we have such a hard time seeing by ourselves. You might not be able to see that you are greedy. You won't have to. Your spouse will point it out for you. Then you can take your sin to the Lord and He can transform you more and more into the likeness of His Son! That's why you should want to get married.

19 Steve Fox, in a random conversation we had one day in 2008.

Marriage reflects Christ's church to the world.

Marriage is built to be a billboard for Jesus. When you are married, you get to display aspects of Jesus Christ to a world that needs to see Jesus Christ; and married couples can do this in a way that unmarried people are simply unable to do. Ephesians says,

> For the husband is the head of the wife even as Christ is the head of the church, his body, and is himself its Savior. Now as the church submits to Christ, so also wives should submit in everything to their husbands. Husbands, love your wives, as Christ loved the church and gave himself up for her, that he might sanctify her, having cleansed her by the washing of water with the word, so that he might present the church to himself in splendor, without spot or wrinkle or any such thing, that she might be holy and without blemish. In the same way husbands should love their wives as their own bodies. He who loves his wife loves himself. For no one ever hated his own flesh, but nourishes and cherishes it, just as Christ does the church, because we are members of his body.[20]

Married people get to show the world how incredible the Church is! They have the unique opportunity to demonstrate to the watching world, in a completely understandable and attractive way, the ideas of mutual submission and cheerful self-sacrifice.[21] Jesus Christ cared for his Church in the most beautiful way possible and people need to see that. Husbands and wives are designed to interact with each other in the same way Jesus did with his bride, the Church.

20 Ephesians 5:23-30
21 Ephesians 5:21

Nowadays, people reject the notion of submitting to another, gender notwithstanding; when you bring male and female into it, the idea becomes downright offensive. But what if Christ-centered marriages got this one right? What if people got to see exactly how attractive those ideas are in their purest form? And what if other people started to see your marriage as a glimpse of an even greater union that leads to salvation? You should want to get married because your marriage can be a billboard for Jesus Christ! That's why you should want to get married.

Sometimes it's really good.

Yes, it's true that many marriages in our society are less than desirable. It's also true that many marriages have two people who practice Christianity and some of those don't fare any better than any of the others that end in disaster. But sometimes it can be really good. When you find those marriages whose partners, out of reverence for Christ, submit to one another,[22] and those whose husbands lead with humility and service, it's refreshing.

Some married people have fun together and enjoy being around each other for a really long time. Some married couples are best friends, even after all the kids move out and graduate from college (and move back in, and then out again – millennials). Some of the marriages that people cultivate are not simple partnerships. They are friendships. Sometimes marriage doesn't end up as a bland co-habitation of convenience, but a lifelong adventure with a lifelong love. Just because most of the marriages you know of don't end this way, or just because many of the marriages you know of end way too soon, doesn't mean the good ones don't exist. They do. What's more is God wants you to have one of the good ones. And He tells us how! God gives great gifts and a long-lasting,

---

22 Ephesians 5:21

God-honoring marriage can be one of those gifts. That is why you should want to get married.

God created marriage to be good.

Going back to Genesis, when God created things, He created them to be good.[23] All of God's creation is still good. None of it is perfect anymore, but it is good. God created land, creatures and man; He created the sun and the moon and the stars, fruits and trees and flowers, earth and sky, night and day.[24] God is a good Father who gives good gifts.[25] He gave humans so many wonderful things. God gave man food, work, a place to live, boundaries, a creative outlet; He gave man so much! The last good gift that God gave man before man rebelled and death entered the world was a spouse. "So the Lord God caused a deep sleep to fall upon the man, and while he slept took one of his ribs and closed up its place with flesh. And the rib that the Lord God had taken from the man he made into a woman and brought her to the man."[26] Marriage was the last pure gift from God to humanity. God preserved this gift for us, even to this day for us to enjoy! That is why you should want to get married.

Don't discount marriage so quickly, especially because your frustration probably isn't with marriage.

Marriage can be a great gift for its participants, a union filled with long-lasting joy. It's designed to reflect Jesus Christ Himself with His bride, the Church. Marriage is a gift from God.

---

23 Genesis 1:4, 10, 12, 18, 21, 25

24 That song from RAs and GAs

25 Matthew 7:11

26 Genesis 2:21-22

I think the people who do lack sexual self-control, but who still don't want to get married, don't want to get married for primarily two reasons: 1) they don't understand what marriage is supposed to be and who marriage is actually for, or 2) they do understand very clearly who is actually involved in marriages and they don't want to deal with the trouble those involved will inevitably bring into the marriage. Sure, sanctification might be a benefit of marriage, but before and during all that wonderful sanctification, there are still just two sinners getting close enough to want to kill each other.

It's the idea that there are two broken people involved in the marriage that might be the most beautiful aspect of marriage. God takes the broken and He fixes it. Fixing broken things is what God does.

This book isn't about marriage. It's about dating. But dating is pointless and even harmful without marriage. The type of marriage that God wants us to have is pointless without the gospel. The gospel is unnecessary without sinners. The next chapter is going to be entirely about the gospel, and the gospel is the real reason why you should want to get married!

The Gospel

If you read this chapter and it changes your life, I honestly don't care if you read the rest of the book.

As simply as I can put it: we are awful, but God's love for us is unending.

THERE ONCE WAS this seventh-grade girl named Meredith who would stop by the church I worked at with her mom once a week after school. Meredith was in the youth group and I was one of the youth leaders. So, like any good youth leader, when Meredith was there I would stop whatever I was doing in order to bug her. I never bothered to ask why her mom was there every week. I presume for a Bible study or something. But every week, Meredith would be waiting in the hallway at the bottom of the stairs until her mother descended and it was time to go. And every week, I would find her. I'm going to share with you a sequence of particular interactions Meredith and I had over a period of several weeks. One small disclaimer: my method of interacting with youth might not be the prescribed method for interacting with youth, but it's the only one I've ever had so it's what I use.

Week one:

Me: Hey Meredith.

Meredith: Hey David.

Me: So, Meredith…

Meredith: Yes, David?

Me: Meredith, do you remember what we talked about at youth group last Sunday?

Meredith: Uhhh… Jesus?

Me: More specifically than that.

Meredith: Well, not really….

Week two:

Me: Hey Meredith.

Meredith: Hey David.

Me: So, Meredith…

Meredith: Yes, David?

Me: Meredith, do you remember what we talked about at youth group last Sunday?

Meredith: Yes! The gospel!

Me: Good!

<wait about 5 seconds>

Me: So, Meredith…

<Meredith rolls her eyes>

Meredith: Yes, David?

Me: What's the gospel?

Meredith: Umm… the first four books of the New Testament.

Me: Well, yes. But what does the word *gospel* mean?

Meredith: Uhhh… I don't know. What does it mean?

Me: I'm not telling you. But I'm probably going to see you Sunday at youth group. You can tell me then.

Meredith: *<rolls her eyes>* Okay.

Week three:

Me: Hey Meredith.

Meredith: Hey David.

Me: So, Meredith…

<rolls eyes… it happens sooner and sooner every time>

Me: Meredith, what does *gospel* mean?

Meredith: I asked my mom. It means "good news."

Me: Good!

<wait about 5 seconds>

Me: So, Meredith…

Meredith: *<rolls eyes>* Yes, David?

Me: What's the good news?

Meredith: The gospel. That's what it means. Good news.

Me: Yeah, but what is this good news?

Meredith: Umm… I don't know, David. *<rolls eyes again>* What is the good news?

Me: I'm not going to tell you. Ask your mom.

Week four:

She didn't show up.

Week five:

Me: Hey Meredith.

Meredith: *<rolls eyes>* Hey David.

Me: So, Meredith…

Meredith: *<deadpan>* The gospel is good news.

Me: Maybe I was going to ask you about your day.

Meredith: *<rolls eyes>* Were you?

Me: No. If the gospel is good news, why is it good news?

Meredith: It's good news because Jesus died on the cross.

Me: Wait!?! WHAT? A guy died? How is a guy dying good news?? I thought you said the news was good?! Why is a guy dying good news?

Meredith: I'm not sure.

Meredith would eventually answer my entire sequence of questions. And by the time she got to high school, she would begin interacting with me without rolling her eyes even once.

I am sure that most church-going middle schoolers don't think deeply enough about the gospel. I imagine that most of us churchgoers regardless of age don't think deeply enough about the gospel, or at least we don't think deeply about the gospel with any regularity. I want to take a moment, for the rest of this chapter, and walk us through the good news about Jesus Christ and why it's good news specifically for anyone who wants to fall in love and get married.

As Meredith will tell you, the word gospel in the Greek is the word *euaggelion*[27] which literally means good tidings, or good

---

27 Strong, J. (1890). *Strong's exhaustive concordance of the Bible*. Abingdon Press.,

news. It is simply that, but it's not nearly that simple. The gospel starts and ends with God, so that's where I will start.

To begin to understand the magnitude of the good news of the gospel, you need to know about God. God created life, the universe and everything. Everything in existence was created by Him and belongs to Him. Everything that remains in existence does so because He allows it.

As I begin to try to express the God of all creation in words, you will have to forgive the reality that the words in our language fall even farther short of how short our capacities for comprehension fall. We can't come close to thinking about it correctly, and as close at that gets, we are incapable of precisely capturing our thoughts with words. The Puritans couldn't even do it. And it certainly doesn't help our case in modern times that we use words like awesome to describe pizza and, well, anything at all. I shall attempt nevertheless.

God is perfect. He is incapable of error. Any aspect of His existence is the very definition of perfection. He is perfectly good. He is perfectly just. He is perfectly righteous. He is perfectly generous. He is perfectly kind. He is perfect.

God is majestic. He is great and impressively beautiful. He has complete sovereignty, complete authority and complete dignity. If awe is truly a concept – Merriam Webster tells us that awe is "an emotion variously combining dread, veneration, and wonder that is inspired by authority or by the sacred or sublime" – then God is truly the only thing in all of existence that is awesome, because anything else by comparison is less than ordinary.[28] Anything else, by comparison, is not worthy of an adjective at all.

God is just. He is perfectly reasonable. He is perfectly moral.

G2098

28 Merriam Webster – awe

He is perfectly proper. He is perfectly right. Not only does he perfectly exhibit righteousness at all times, He is righteousness itself.

If you have ever thought about God and your heart rate didn't increase; if you have ever thought about God and your reaction wasn't a 10 on a scale of 1 to 10, then your concept of God isn't as in-depth or complete as it needs to be. Thus is the nature of God. Only bit by bit (and at His pleasure) will we come to see Him more and more clearly. Thankfully, however, He gives us enough understanding to be able to grasp what we need at any given moment. His perfection matters very much when we understand the gospel is good news because of our imperfection.

One of the biggest mistakes people like me, who spend large amounts of time talking to others (particularly people under the age of 30) about theological things, make is that we are too much in a hurry. We are in so much of a hurry for you to know God and know salvation, that we often don't give the people we're talking to a chance to grasp the gravity and irreconcilability of their transgressions. The more deeply aware someone is of his or her rebellion against God, the more room there is to see the need for a solution to an impossible situation.

We were designed in the image of God to perfectly reflect all the character qualities of our Creator, God. When we do not operate in the way we were designed, we are dishonoring the most powerful, wholly perfect Being. God wants and deserves for all His creation to honor Him with every fiber of our being, every moment of the day. When we choose wrong in any way (deed, speech, or thought) our rebellion, however small, is against His supreme authority and perfection. Any imperfect act we commit is called sin.

When we sin, it is a huge problem. God, as the founder of the universe and the inventor and sustainer of everything that is morally right, is righteous and therefore cannot ignore that part of Himself when faced with unrighteousness. When anyone transgresses absolute perfection, the just recourse for that person is death. If a feudal peasant were to walk into the home of his feudal lord and slap the lady of the manor, surely the lord of the manor would punish him severely. If that same peasant were to walk into the court of the king and slap the monarch himself, that slap would probably be the last voluntary act that peasant ever takes. I imagine the king would not hesitate in proclaiming, "Off with his head!" When you rebel against the King, your punishment will be fierce.

When God, who is responsible for upholding the very existence of morality and righteousness because He is morality and righteousness, intersects with unrighteousness of any kind, the just punishment is the annihilation of that thing. When we sin against God, because He is SO holy, because He is absolutely perfect, how can He uphold His perfection and allow our imperfection at the same time? He doesn't have the easy choice of simply forgiving us and forgetting about it. The very existence of justice and morality hang in the balance. A really smart guy said it like this once, "If the just and eternal ethical order that is the very foundation of a moral universe rivets together sin and its due reward, how can He who is that very order, separate them, and yet be its God? Forgiveness to man is the plainest of duties; to God it is the profoundest of problems."[29]

So, everyone involved has a problem. We have a problem with the unforgiveness of God because that leads to the thing we earned, which is our death. God has a problem with forgiveness because the very idea of not making right a wrong that has been committed challenges His authority and very character as God. Our rebellion causes this problem for both us and God, and it's a

29 Simpson, Patrick Carnegie (1901). The Fact of Christ, London: Hodder and Stoughton. p 109.

huge problem with eternal ramifications. It is the profoundest of problems, indeed.

When we sin, we incur this debt whose very price is our lives. There is nothing we can do by ourselves to erase the black mark we created when we ruined the perfect record we had with God. In fact, it's even worse than that. When we try to do things to make up for our sin, we end up just sinning more. It's like you are trying to get mud off a window and all you have is a towel completely covered in mud. If you think you can earn your way back into favor with God, you do not understand how egregious your rebellion is, nor do you understand God's perfection. There is nothing you can do to fill the hole your sin created. Being a good person, doing good deeds, being sincere, practicing a religion, even saving another person's life at risk of your own – all of these things are nice, but they are just moving dirt around with more dirt. Even worshiping God isn't enough to cover the mark of our sin. We might proclaim Him publicly, but we deny Him in our hearts.[30]

But God is also a God of mercy.

Here is the good news. God figured out how to remain God without having to kill us (and I say, "figured out," but He knew the whole time). God required a propitiation. Propitiation is just a fancy word for appeasement.[31] Appeasement is just a fancy word for bringing peace to someone by giving a thing that is desired. It's just us and God in this transaction, and we can't afford the propitiation. Only God is able to present this peace to us. And He did. This is good news for everyone involved.

The cost was high for God, but it was impossible for us, therefore God demonstrated His great love for us by paying our debt of

30 Stott, John (2012). *The Cross of Christ*, InterVarsity Press.

31 Kemp, Thomas. "Psalm 51." Summer Psalms. Summer Refuge, 17 July 2016, Baton Rouge.

sin for us. In the economy of a just God, the cost of sin is a life. So, God decided to go to earth in human form, in the form of a man named Jesus. One of Jesus' closest friends gives the best explanation of what happened, so I'll defer to John.

> In the beginning was the Word, and the Word was with God, and the Word was God. He was in the beginning with God. All things were made through him, and without him was not anything made that was made. In him was life, and the life was the light of men.... And the Word became flesh and dwelt among us, and we have seen his glory, glory as of the only Son from the Father, full of grace and truth.[32]

God came to earth in human form and lived with us. He was exposed to a myriad of opportunities to sin against God, but His desire was always the will of God, so He never sinned. He referred to God as "Father" and demonstrated perfect love. Jesus embodied all of God's attributes while on earth. He was full of truth and grace.

Perfect Jesus perfectly reflected a perfect God, and then He chose to give up His life in exchange for our lives. He was brutally beaten and punished after having done nothing wrong. He was bruised and teased and abused, wrongfully accused by people who had no excuse. He was hung on a cross to die by torturous asphyxiation, which He did. He died on a cross to solve the problem of God's forgiveness. By dying, He paid the death penalty for our sin. Then after three days in a tomb, He did the unimaginable. He rose from the dead. He literally defeated death, both for Himself and everyone who would believe in Him. When He rose from the

---

32 John 1:1-5, 14

dead, after having never sinned His whole life, He demonstrated that He was at His very essence, God Himself.

Because of Jesus' demonstration of Deity, He freely gives us His image, His Spirit, and His right to be with God. Once again, John says it best: "But to all who did receive him, who believed in his name, he gave the right to become children of God, who were born, not of blood nor of the will of the flesh nor of the will of man, but of God."[33]

It is good news that God figured out the answer to His problem and ours. It is good news that He also provided the answer to the problem. It's even better news that since God paid the full price of our sin debt, we don't have to figure out how to pay for it ourselves. In fact, He won't let us pay for it! If we don't take it freely, we can't take it at all! It's grace. It can make us uncomfortable because we are getting something extremely valuable that we neither deserve nor can afford.

Then after we have received that incredible gift of grace, and only after, we get to choose to respond in an appropriate manner, by freely giving the thing Jesus paid such a high price for: our lives. It's only when we align our lives with His that we can find true life. Aligning our lives with His is where all the desires we have in life will be fulfilled in a way that is wholly satisfying to us and honoring to God. Day by day, God shapes our desires into His holiness. It is in God's holiness where life will provide joy. It is in God's holiness where we will find what we look for in relationships, and in God's holiness where we find the type of relationships that are honoring to God and fulfilling to us.

Jesus died on the cross and rose from the dead so that we can experience God's holiness. Nothing else in this book works if you have not trusted and anchored your life to the fact that Jesus is the

33 John 1:12-13

Son of God, the literal essence of God in the flesh, and that He came to earth from God's presence, lived a perfect life and died a perfect, blameless death on a cross only to have God raise Him from the dead on the third day. People who operate in this truth live radically different lives than people who don't. If your life has been altered by an encounter with Jesus, the Son of God, and you want to find out how it's possible to date and marry while living that radically different life, keep reading. If not, maybe read this chapter again.[34]

For the next few chapters, we are going to look at the current dating landscape. We will analyze what goes on and why our current reality is not anchored in truth. Then after that, we will look at what reality might look like if the dating landscape *were* anchored in truth. Spoiler alert: it's better.

---

34 Also read the Letter of Paul to the Romans

The Anatomy of Dating

LET'S TALK ABOUT dating. If you have been of dating age for any period of time, you probably know that dating is not a simple thing to describe. If you are not of the millennial generation but have been in a position to listen to millennials and post-millennials talk about dating or observe any of their attempts to date, you may be a little confused at the terms used to describe something that used to be so simple. That's why I'm going to take a few moments to describe what we are going to be talking about, just so that we are all working with the same definitions and talking about the same things at the same time.

I'll never forget the first time I heard about the concept of "going out." I was in first grade. Steven started going out with Amy. I didn't know what it meant. They explained it means that they like each other. Well, I liked a lot of people. They explained you have to pick one person and that it has to be a girl. Well, I liked Emory. So I started going out with Emory. That one didn't last very long, a day or two, maybe. It worked out well for us because we didn't even break up with each other. I think we both kind of forgot we were "going out." If I have to recommend a way to end a relationship, that would be it. You both just kind of forget, and then you get to remain friends until one of you switches schools in fourth grade. Come to think of it, I'm not sure anyone explained the concept of breaking up to first-grade me.

In middle school, a lot more people started going out with one another. Those relationships didn't last much longer than the ones in elementary school, but they sure did mean a lot more. When you grow up and become an adult, you remember that those relationships happened. Thankfully I was spared going out with anyone in middle school, but I still remember a few of the pairings: Jason and Kim, Tehmi and Brandy, Chuck and Brittany, Chuck and Piper, Chuck and Jessica.... I don't remember a lot about those middle school relationships, but I do remember one thing clearly: exactly zero of the pairs actually went out anywhere to any places together except maybe the cafeteria or the playground. I guess Steven and Amy weren't there to explain to everyone that going out was supposed to entail *going out*.

You can have a relationship with someone without being in a relationship with someone. In fact, you're not in a relationship with most of the people with whom you have a relationship. The only way this makes sense is if you're not thinking about it. You can be talking about having a relationship with someone you're not in a relationship with and with whom you're not talking. This will make complete sense to basically anyone who has lived in/ through the contemporary millennial generation. It shouldn't make sense. But it does.

Here's my point: sometimes going out means going out, but sometimes it doesn't. Sometimes dating means dating, but sometimes it doesn't. Sometimes talking means talking, but sometimes it doesn't. And having a relationship can sometimes mean being in a relationship, but not always. Talking about dating can cause a migraine unless we have clear definitions for all our terms. Let's start from the very beginning.

Modern dating happens in phases. The first phase is the talking phase. Talking, to millennials, isn't actually talking, or at least it's not simply talking. Mike's[35] is the top explanation for "talking" on *UrbanDictionary.com*; he defines it as, "When two people are not exclusive with each other nor have established what they are as a couple, but have some sort of relationship."[36] Mike's definition does a great job of capturing the essence of the concept in that his definition isn't very precise, which oddly fits the idea of "talking" because it, in and of itself, is not a very precise thing. Talking is when a guy and girl consciously acknowledge that they might possibly have a mutual romantic interest and they are actively moving towards establishing a committed romantic relationship. I think the two most important aspects of the talking phase are that both people are aware of the others' interest, and neither person feels any justifiable feelings of obligation towards the other person.

If enough time passes and both people agree that they want to continue to develop interest in one another, they can begin dating. This is also the point at which the two begin "going out," which is the same thing as becoming official or dating. Depending on the age of the participants, they may, in fact, have not been on one or more of what we will define as a "date." When two people are dating one another, they mutually agree to limit their affections, gestures and thoughts of romance, and sometimes personal interaction with the opposite sex to their chosen other.

This book is directed towards Christians, and so I will be skipping the co-habitation phase which is a popular next step for modern contemporary relationships. There are some non-Christians who skip the step of co-habitation and there are some Christians who do choose to engage in co-habitation before

35 Mike has 1523 entries on Urban Dictionary.com. I think that makes Mike an internet expert. Urban Dictionary: Author Mike, Retrieved August 20, 2018; http://www.urbandictionary.com/author.php?author=Mike

36 Urban Dictionary: Talking, by Mike, June 16, 2014, Retrieved: September 30, 2016; http://www.urbandictionary.com/define.php?term=talking

marriage, but because this is still frowned upon in Christian circles and engaging in this step doesn't technically change the relationship status, I will not be addressing this.

When enough time passes and if dating goes well, the next step is engagement or betrothal. You might think engagement is pretty standard, but it's not. For some people, the point of engagement is to plan a wedding and get married. For others, the point of engagement is to increase the intensity and scrutiny of the relationship to ensure that this person is the one with whom they want to spend the rest of their lives. If all goes as expected for both of the two engaged people, the engagement ends at their wedding.

The last phase of relationship is marriage. This is the only step whose definition is perfectly clear. You get to be with the same person until one of you dies! Of course, with the advent of open marriages and divorce and remarriage, even marriage isn't as simple as we'd like it to be. However, everything in this paragraph is either right on the edge of, or beyond the scope of this book, so I will not be addressing any of that.

Let's take a closer look at the two problem children of the dating spectrum, talking and dating. Because the talking phase shares many of the same attributes as dating, only dating is more formal and serious while the talking phase is more casual, we will henceforth call the talking phase "casual dating." Plus, we now get to eliminate any unnecessary confusion by reclaiming the word "talking" to exclusively mean expressing or exchanging ideas by means of spoken words.[37]

---

37 Merriam-Webster, talk

Casual Dating

As previously defined, casual dating begins when a guy and a girl begin to express mutual interest in one another. It usually begins immediately after one of the two participants has asked the other to do something together and after that thing is complete, there is still interest. At this point in the relationship progression, the two participants don't have titles for each other. Two hundred years ago, she might call him a suitor, but that term is long gone. (I wish we would bring it back. C'mon, *UrbanDictionary.com*). She might describe him as "a guy I went out with," but there are no official titles. After a slow start, the volume of text messages sent between the two will most probably increase dramatically. Most of the messages will be pointless and have zero content. But there will be texting.

This is when the two begin to establish rapport with each other. Typically, if things are progressing, there will be inside jokes, possible future plans, but nothing definite, unless it's definite. Even the definiteness of things isn't defined in this stage. This casual dating stage will probably last two weeks or so.[38] If it goes any longer than this, one of the people has moved out of the stage and the other person probably doesn't know it yet. Don't worry, they will.

There are no rules in this stage. For instance, if you start casually dating someone and a holiday occurs during this time, you do not have to acknowledge the holiday.[39] If the other person happens

---

38 Unless it goes longer – it's hard defining something that has as one of its core tenants a lack of definition.

39 If you do get the other person a gift for Christmas or something, it had better not be very expensive; also, unless you're sure they're into you, it had better not be romantic. Cute is okay. And if the holiday is Valentine's Day, just pretend it doesn't even exist.

to get sick, you don't have to buy them soup.[40] You don't even have to acknowledge their sickness in any way that would be any different than any other person you heard was sick. In fact, though it can be seen as petty, them getting sick is enough reason to stop casually dating that person.

At the beginning of the casual dating stage, you are under no obligation to only express interest to that one person. The other person has no right to expect that he or she is the only other person with whom you are casually dating. However, if you do happen to find out the other person is pursuing someone else, you can end the casual relationship if you aren't okay with exploring interest in someone else at the same time.

Any expectations that occur in this stage of the relationship are self-imposed. After going out one or two times, there is almost always no obligation or expectation to go out again. Neither person has to text back. Neither person has to call back. Unless the guy says, "I'll call you" after a date or an outing, there is no valid expectation that he will call.[41]

If one person goes more than a few days without communicating, it probably means the relationship is over. If either person says no to an invitation more than twice in a row without suggesting an alternative, it probably means the relationship is over. Conversely, any type of romantic physical affection is a sign that the casual dating stage is over – and it may be the end of the entire relationship if the expressed physical affection is unrequited. But maybe not. If the relationship ends during the casual dating stage, it is not an official breakup because you weren't officially dating.

---

40 I think bringing soup to a sick person is a very kind thing to do. But it's possible that bringing the person soup can be interpreted as "too much" and can cause the sick person to end it as soon as he is well enough to do so. So if you want to bring soup, be sure to get permission first.

41 If you tell someone you're going to call them later, call them later, regardless of whether you are trying to date the person or not. That's just common courtesy.

There used to be this thing called the DTR – define the relationship. This was the conversation that takes place so that both people know they are no longer casually dating and are now officially dating. This is the same conversation where if one person is tired of casual dating and wants to start dating but the other doesn't, the relationship usually ends. A lot of people don't call this step the DTR anymore, but it still happens. After the DTR, the relationship is either over or you are boyfriend and girlfriend.[42]

So that's casual dating.

Now, let's define dating. And once again, I'm talking about Christian dating – so no sex.

Title Requirements

Once you successfully make it through the casual dating stage, you are now official! This is the stage in the relationship where you first get titles. "This is my girlfriend, [name]" you would say to someone who is meeting her for the first time. As soon as you are official, you are expected to introduce the other person as your boyfriend or girlfriend. Some people will get upset at you if you don't acknowledge your status with them. Also, you are not under any circumstances allowed to simply call your boyfriend or girlfriend a "friend" to someone else unless you have discussed it beforehand.

---

42 This step isn't that simple, either. Sometimes if the communication is bad enough, one of the parties can attempt to end the relationship unsuccessfully. When this happens, future DTRs are in order with generally increasing frustration of both parties every time.

Time Requirements

You have to spend time with your significant other. Obviously, you should want to spend time with the person you're dating, but whether you want to spend time with them or not, you *have* to spend time with them. When you are dating, you are no longer allowed to live through a holiday without discussing it with your boyfriend/girlfriend. You don't have to do everything with them, but there is an expectation that you let them know all the things you're going to do without them.

You have to get special permission to spend one-on-one time with someone of the opposite sex, unless it's for school or work.[43] Maybe not at the very beginning, but eventually, there will come the expectation that if you go and do something fun, the person with whom you are in a relationship has the right of first refusal. Also, ironically, the longer you're in a relationship, you lose the right to refuse invitations free of charge.[44] Hopefully, it's a long time before you want to say no to an invitation, so you don't have to be concerned about not doing what the other person wants, but it's only a matter of time.

Length Requirements

There is no set length of time that people can or must date. It can be as short as a few days or several years. A lot of times, the length of the relationship is dictated by outside factors; you don't want to break up, but you can't get married while you're in school because your parents will stop supporting you, or you don't want

---

43 Depending on the level of dysfunction of the relationship or the level of insecurity of the other person, even school or work doesn't exempt you from getting permission first.

44 You don't have to go to the event, but if not you are going to be talking/fighting about it later.

to get distracted from your schooling, or you have a military commitment or any number of things. Sometimes one person is ready to commit long term much sooner than the other person and you have to wait until both of you are ready. Some people date indefinitely without specific intent to ever move beyond the dating phase, but most Christian don't find themselves in this category.

Once you are dating, there are only two ways to end the relationship;[45] you either get married or you break up. We'll talk about marriage later. While you are dating, you can still end the relationship any time you want to, but you usually have to have a conversation about it. The conversation usually ends up being a series of conversations. Breaking up is hard for both parties, but it is especially for the person who doesn't initiate it. Both people are going to need closure, and usually the person who initiated the breakup has had much more time to process, and probably at his or her preferred pace (which helps a lot) so when the breakup actually happens, the initiator is much more prepared.[46]

Other Requirements

I heard a Christian speaker named Jared Herd talk about relationships at a Christian camp one summer.[47] He said that relationships have six areas: emotional, physical, spiritual, social, intellectual and commitment. He told us to think of them on a scale from one to ten, one being very low and ten being very high. Jared said that the key is to have balance. He said if you're at an emotional eight and an intellectual two, then that balance is unhealthy. If you're at a physical level of eight and a commitment level of one, that too is unhealthy. He said that the key to a healthy relationship is balance

---

45 Without one of you being abducted by aliens, *et al.*

46 This is true even when both people can honestly say they saw the end coming.

47 BigStuf Camps, summer of 2008

at all six levels at once. When I heard him say this at the Christian camp that summer, I thought it made a lot of sense. Now, I still think it makes sense – I just think it's wrong.[48]

Generally, people who are dating or courting one another in this contemporary millennial Christian culture are going to interact in these ways. Not every relationship is going to look exactly the same, but they will almost all have most of the elements we talked about up here. If you are living in Western culture, I suspect nothing you read has surprised you. You might have known some of the things we talked about by a different name, but without specifics this is what people who are engaged in contemporary relationships are experiencing.

There is one particular aspect inside the realm of dating that needs a bit more attention than I have given in this chapter, so we will have to dive a little deeper still before we can talk about how to commence acquiring a spouse without making it harder for yourself than you have to. This aspect gets a lot of attention from most people and for good reason: because it is very important. I'm referring to sex. Let's talk about it.

---

48 My vehement disagreement with Jared will be explained in later chapters, particularly when we discuss commitment.

Let's Talk About Sex

IT DOESN'T MAKE sense to have a book about dating if we're not going to talk about sex. If you don't think so, keep reading and I think you'll see that the two are inextricably linked. For some people, sex is the only reason why people date in the first place.

Christians believe that sex is something that is reserved for marriage. I'm going to talk about why God designed it this way and why it's better for us this way (whether you believe in God or not). We are going to analyze the way the world looks at sex in comparison to highlight God's brilliance.

Therefore, there is no condemnation.

Hopefully, when this chapter is completed, you will be convinced that sex is something that makes the most sense to be reserved exclusively for two people who are in a marriage relationship; however, I want to take a minute here (and also at the end of this chapter) to talk to the person who is not married, but has already had sex. So many times, guilt and shame and feelings of unworthiness accompany people who are in a relationship with Jesus but have had a sexual past. The fact that our lives are in Jesus Christ means that we need not carry guilt and shame from our past with us. We are told in God's word that condemnation has no place in the life of a Christian.[49] Sadly though, many times it is the church who fans the flame of guilt. If you have ever been made to feel this way by a church or a minister or a priest, or by a well-meaning parent trying to teach you to live biblically, on behalf of the church, I apologize. Please remember that Jesus came to die on behalf of only the people who have fallen short of God's standards. If you have had sex, you are no worse a Christian because of it than the Christ-followers who have sinned against God in other ways, but not that way. You are no less worthy of God's love than anyone else. You are no less eligible for God's grace than anyone else. You are no less deserving of Christ's love than anyone else. You are no less deserving or eligible to have a happy marriage that honors God. We are going to talk about the perils and dangers of using sex outside of God's design, but you need to know that you are exactly as valuable to God as anyone else who has ever lived. And just because you may have already messed up sexually in the past, this chapter is still for you.

What Sex Is

Sex might be something anyone can learn without instructions, but just like with everything worth talking about in this book, we are going to have to define what we are talking about so that we have a common understanding as we move forward.

Sex is Powerful

Sex is one of the most powerful phenomena in the universe. Just think about this. The possibility of a living, breathing human being that did not exist anywhere before can be created as a result

---

49 Romans 8:1

of sex. But even beyond what may or may not happen because of having sex, sex itself is an enormously powerful thing. Sex also has some powerful spiritual implications, but I will talk about that more in depth in the following sections.

What the World Says About Sex

One of the biggest problems we face, however, is that the world doesn't see sex with the gravity it commands. Media, movies, television, commercials all teach us lessons about sex, and they are all wrong. But we are an attentive audience and we are always in class. The classes are engaging, comprehensive, and convincing. Now for the Christians who have good biblical teaching, we can spot some of the obvious falsehoods, but it is virtually impossible for us to catch them all. For now, I will cover some of the bigger ones.

Sex Lessons from Popular Culture

Sex is a physical act, but it's not just physical.[50] We're not going to pick on any one particular movie or TV show, but we don't have to because the examples are myriad. We see sex portrayed as a simple physical act. It's something people do when they are attracted to one another. Media tells us that sex is something we can do with someone, and then some time later another someone, and then a little while later another someone and there are no major repercussions. Often times, sex is something that characters will brag about for which they give statistics. In the 2011 comedy film *What's your Number*, we see the entire premise is that whereas sex is something you are expected to do regardless of your marital status, too many

---

50 Stanley, Andy (2015). "Designer Sex" The New Rules of Love, Sex and Dating. North Point Community Church.

partners eventually make it harder to get married.[51] Media tells us that we are to be entertained by the multiple sexual exploits of fictional characters. We can laugh about it because sex is no big deal. Sex is just a fun, somewhat special physical act. Popular television programs show us by example that sex is just something you do when you are in a relationship and it is something of little consequence in the grand scheme of things.[52] [53] [54]

Sex isn't just physical.

The problem is that sex isn't just physical. That's why the effects of sexual abuse are so much worse than simply getting beat up. When someone is beaten up many times after the wounds heal, they can eventually "get over it," but one act of sexual abuse can ruin a person's life forever. We know sex is not just physical because of the shame that is attached to acts like molestation and rape. If you are robbed or beat up, you just report it to the authorities, but when the assault is sexual, the victims sometimes feel so much shame that he or she will not report the assault for weeks, months or sometimes even years, if ever. If sex were just physical, the devastation so many people experience because of it would not be warranted. If sex were just physical, childhood sexual abuse would not have the same lifelong effects for a victim well into adulthood that will sometimes take years to overcome. If sex were just physical, the harm people suffer for it would be just like any other physical harm, but it's not. Sex is a physical act, but it's not just a

---

51 IMDB – What's Your Number? (2011), *http://www.imdb.com/title/tt0770703/*

52 IMDB – "Seinfeld" The Yada Yada (TV Episode 1997), *http://www.imdb.com/title/tt0697814/*

53 IMDB – "Friends" The One Where Monica Gets A Roommate (TV Episode 1994), *http://www.imdb.com/title/tt0583459/*

54 IMDB – "Sex and the City" Sex and the City (TV Episode 1998), *http://www.imdb.com/title/tt0698663/*

physical act. We would be wise not to treat it like it is just physical in any context.

Sex isn't just intercourse.

Sex is intercourse, but it isn't just intercourse. There are many, many things that people can do that fall on the spectrum of sexual activity. For everything we will discuss later to make sense now and later, we have to agree about this one. We must recognize that all forms of sexual relations are more than physical. They all have emotional and spiritual implications that we cannot ignore.

The Bible tells us to abstain from sexual immorality.[55] I am positing that sexual immorality is engaging in any type of sexual activity at a time that is not endorsed by Scripture. Most Christians can agree that sexual intercourse outside of marriage is not allowed as prescribed in the Bible. What a lot of Christians can't seem to agree on is what other types of intimate interactions aren't prohibited for non-married people by the Bible. Christians can't seem to agree on where to draw boundaries.

Boundaries

Christians address sexual boundaries in all the wrong ways. But you, oh reader, are in luck because starting now, you get to get it right! If you have been a Christian for a while, you will have heard most of the boundary drawing methods I'm about to discuss.

When people begin dating, they want to experience intimacy with the person they are dating, but they also want to do the right thing in God's eyes. They quickly discover that sexual intimacy is on a continuum. There is a presumption that on the mild end of the spectrum (*e.g.* looking into your boyfriend's eyes or holding

---

55 1 Thessalonians 4:3

hands) there is nothing inherently wrong with those acts, but on the far end of the spectrum there are things that are inherently wrong. The big idea then is to figure out what things on the far end of the intimacy spectrum aren't okay and to stay away from them, but to be okay with the things that are okay. In figuring out which things are and aren't okay, it's usually phrased like this: "How far is too far?"

How far is too far?

People have been trying to figure out the answer to the question "How far is too far?" ever since Christians started using dating to find a mate. I've heard lots of different ways to go about addressing this question.

One of the most prevalent ways people (especially younger people) deal with this question is to not consider it until it's too late. Once they've gone too far, they can recognize it from personal experience. The problem with this is the knowledge gained is never worth the price paid and the baggage acquired.

I've been in Christian circles where people got this advice:[56] use accountability and your conscience beforehand to decide what you and the other person are comfortable with. Discuss with the other person what is acceptable and have people in your account-ability group hold you to your standards. This one doesn't work because our hearts are deceitful and wicked[57] and we can convince ourselves of anything. Also, the longer you are with someone, the easier it will be to be more comfortable with more things. Using your personal comfort and convictions are surely better than not

---

56 There have been a few times when I was in the cohort of leaders giving the advice.

57 Jeremiah 17:9

deciding anything beforehand, but it's not going to lead you to where you eventually will want to be.

If you've read any of the good Christian dating books by now, you have almost certainly heard this advice: when you ask "How far is too far?" you're asking the wrong question. And if you're asking the wrong question, you will never get the right answer.[58] The question you need to ask instead is, how can I most honor God in my relationship with the way I display affection to my boyfriend or girlfriend. This is *by far* the best way of addressing the topic so far, but it's wrong too.

Let me explain: yes, it is good for us to not focus on the physicality, but instead focus on God. Yes, you should strive for holiness in the way you interact with the person you're dating. In everything you do, strive for holiness; strive to honor God. But that is not the standard you want to adopt if you want to get the results in dating you actually want.

How should I view sex?

Here is my advice, and I am sure there will be a lot of people who don't like it. But I will explain and you still might not like it. However, I think you'll be hard-pressed to disagree. Sexual activity is reserved for marriage. All sexual activity is reserved for marriage. If it's sexual, don't do it. But what about holding hands? And what about a side hug? And what about a non-side hug that only lasts for half a second? And what about a kiss on the forehead? On the cheek? What about a high five? And what about legalism, legalist? Are we about to try and squelch our freedom in Christ?

As we will discuss more in-depth in a subsequent chapter, sexual activity is any activity done with a romantic or sexual

---

58 Which actually isn't true, though you will be exponentially less likely to find the right answer by asking the wrong questions.

intent. That intent is why trying to categorize certain acts in one category or another is an impossibly fruitless endeavor. Sometimes, the intent of your heart makes all the difference. Also, sometimes, God is the only one who can accurately divine your intent. You can even confuse yourself about your motives sometimes. I would like to say that some actions are totally safe from ever being sexual in nature, but intent is a fickle thing. I have never seen, nor can I imagine, a high five done with sexual intent, but I'm not you.

I need to be clear about this. I'm not talking about being dogmatic about sin. I'm not saying that making out before marriage is a sin. It certainly can be, but I'm not saying that it always is, or it is when you, in particular, do it. I'm not saying that regular kissing is a sin. It's not. I'm not saying that back rubs or hand-holding or any of those things are sin.[59] I mean, they can be, but anything can be. Supersizing your fries or not ordering fries at all can be sin. This advice is not[60] about holiness or righteousness. This advice is about making it easier for you to end up where you actually want to end up, with the person you actually want to be with.

All PDA comes with baggage.

Every act on the sexual spectrum has components that are beyond being simply physical. Emotions are tied into a kiss in a way that emotions are absent from a handshake with someone you just met. Whether it is kissing, or sensual hugs, using his shoulder as a head-rest and falling asleep while the two of you are watching a movie, or even holding hands romantically, there is an element of emotion; it won't do me any good to try to create an exhaustive list, but a list isn't the point. We need to understand that amorous physical interaction with another person *always* has baggage that comes

---

59 They're not

60 not necessarily

46

with it. That baggage is what makes trying to discern whether the person you're with is in fact the person you actually want to be with forever more difficult. Also, the baggage you acquire might move with you from relationship to relationship.

Conclusion

Displaying intimate affection with another person can be gratifying and satisfying and fun. These actions can communicate affection more clearly and with more impact than words or gifts or just about anything else. However, intimate affection always leaves an impact on both people, many times for much longer than the length of the intimate relationship, no matter the act. This is why we must be careful with whom we decide to express our feelings with intimate displays that fall on the sexual spectrum. You might think you're less affected by some things, and you might be right. Or you might not have a chance to realize how wrong you are until months or years later when it is much more complicated and difficult to find needed resolution or to do anything about it.

If you do have baggage: bad memories, resentment towards another person, scarring of your soul, anything – you are not beyond redemption. You can't always get rid of all the consequences of past actions, but God can heal you completely. He can make you completely whole, even before Jesus comes back. God can redeem even your worst of mistakes. God is in the redemption business.

Now we are going to look at some of the other problematic aspects of current dating practice. I think it's good to take an honest look at the way we as a culture are currently doing things, because the way we are doing things makes everything harder. Things shouldn't be harder than they have to be. There is a better way.

The Problem with Security and Pursuit

THE IDEA OF security in a dating relationship is one of the most dangerous aspects of the way contemporary Christian culture presents dating. It has the potential to get in the way of someone finding a truly secure, healthy relationship as much as any other effect of dating. Even so, the idea of security is appealing, as it should be. Nobody wants to be insecure. Nobody wants to be in a relationship that is insecure. Everyone wants security. A married couple must have security in their relationship if it is going to be healthy. We were designed for security and stability. So, what's so bad about having security in a dating relationship? Great question. Let's talk about it.

Marriage is permanent. Dating is temporary. Dating might lead to something more permanent than dating, but the dating itself is temporary. Something that is definitionally temporary cannot provide any type of lasting security. Exposing the deepest and most fragile parts of our spirits and emotions to another human being in a context that is temporary is unwise. No matter the situation, if we are dealing with another imperfect human, the potential for emotional hurt and devastation will be present. Two imperfect people within a secure relationship situation is a much wiser proposition than two imperfect people in a relational situation that is not secure. When we realize that our situation is insecure, we are much less likely to behave emotionally as if we were secure and also less likely to expose ourselves to unnecessary hurt. It is irrational and unwise to express feelings of security inside of something, like dating, that is inherently insecure.

Dating definitely has its perks. One thing that always seems to appeal to people in the dating world is the idea that you don't have to figure out who to do stuff with. Do you have a winter formal dance or some other event coming up? While you might not know what you're going to wear or where you're going to eat or a thousand other details about the event, if you have a boyfriend, you don't have to be concerned with how to find a date. If you are already dating someone you never have to be afraid of going alone. If you already have the answer to the question of who, you get to focus more on all the other questions. Also, you get to unapologetically play matchmaker with your other friends who aren't already dating someone – and that's always fun.

You don't have to get nervous about finding someone with whom to attend events. The idea of being rejected is essentially removed from the equation. Depending on how long you've been dating, you can even do nothing and have company while you do it. If you are trying to list virtues and values of the way everyone else dates, this one would almost be a no-brainer in the way the contemporary millennial Christian culture gets this one right... except for the tradeoff.

One of the negatives that comes from this feeling of security is what it does to pursuit. Women want to be pursued by men and men need to pursue women. Each was innately designed to operate this way. But the fallen nature of people has caused the impulses of men and women to dampen and get muddled, or even switch. Pursuit is hard for men and waiting for that pursuit is hard for women.

Before a man has a girlfriend, he has to find her and pursue her. However, once they are in a dating relationship, the man knows she is his, so he no longer has to pursue her. There is no need to chase something that has already been caught. When a guy has a girlfriend, he doesn't have to put forth much effort, or he gets to choose when he wants to put forth effort. He doesn't have to try to win her if he thinks he's already won.

However, a man needs to pursue. A man might not want to pursue because it's scary and because it takes effort and because it probably means less time for video games, but he needs to. Here is the thing about pursuit: in the type of relationship that you really want to be in, the man never stops pursuing his beloved, ever. From the moment he decides to pursue her 'til death do us part, a man needs to actively pursue her affections.

In the contemporary millennial Christian culture there is a pursuit, but it only lasts in its purest form until the guy gets her to agree to be his girlfriend. After this, the nature of the pursuit changes if it doesn't completely disappear. The way a man goes about trying to keep his girlfriend happy is different than the way he goes about trying to overcome the uncertainty of where her affections will ultimately rest.

When a guy achieves the status of having a girlfriend, his strongest motivation is taken away. He loses the mystery of what it will actually take to win her affections. When a girl agrees to exclusively date one guy, she is tacitly giving him permission to relax a little bit in his pursuit. The only way that permission isn't given is if the guy thinks he is in danger of losing her, and that's never healthy. The fear of losing something that belongs to you is jealousy and jealousy is not the motivation we want driving our relationships. We do not want jealousy to have anything to do with any part of our relationships if what we are looking for is healthy relationships.

Engaging in an earnest pursuit before and until marriage makes a great difference in the health of a marriage. If men build a deep relational foundation of pursuing the woman who will be his wife, once they are married, it will be much easier for that pursuit to continue. If a man has practiced pursuing a woman over a long period of time, but has never done so with the express or implicit idea that the pursuit can end, it will benefit her and him later on in a marriage because he will be much less likely to stop and his pursuit of her will be more refined and practiced. Pursuing someone well is a skill that can be developed with practice.

Complacency in the pursuit of a spouse is something men and women who are married need to guard against because it welcomes in strife and heartache. The husband's job will be much easier if he hasn't been able to practice complacency or even entertain the idea of complacency at any point before he is married. A man needs to demonstrate planning, effort and desire to any woman whose heart he desires to have. Men need to work for her affections – and they would be well served never to stop.

So, does this mean that we should encourage females to play hard to get? Absolutely not. She shouldn't be playing hard to get. She actually *should* be hard to get. Please keep in mind, in terms of hard to get, the thing that is being given and gotten is giving your heart. Your heart is way too precious to play games with or to give away to someone who hasn't truly earned it; you should give your heart only once with the idea of death being the only thing that separates you. Your affections are too valuable, and your heart is too fragile for anything else. Anything else and you will be teaching your heart how to be guarded in the wrong ways. Experiencing a breakup or a broken heart is pain from which you should want to protect yourself. A breakup comes with excruciating pain and one way or another you will protect yourself from that pain. You might stop giving guys a chance. You might limit your vulnerability while you're in a relationship. But here's the thing: you need to limit your vulnerability. It's the only prudent thing. It's the only way to avoid deep pain that leaves deep scars.

There is a famous TED talk by this social worker named Brené Brown about vulnerability. She talks about connection and how vulnerability is a necessary part of being in a healthy relationship. Brown talks about how trying to guard against vulnerability is one of the most effective things we can do to prevent true connections with people; if we practice preventing getting hurt by avoiding vulnerability, it has some dangerous consequences. If you do go back and listen to the entire TED talk, Brown says some misleading things that reinforce the way our culture goes about making relationships harder, but she also says some brilliant things about vulnerability.

> We live in a vulnerable world. And one of the ways we deal with it is we numb vulnerability. And I think there's evidence – we are the most in debt, obese, addicted and medicated adult cohort in U.S. history. The problem is – and I learned this from the research – you can't selectively numb the bad stuff. You can't say, "Here's the bad stuff: here's vulnerability, here's grief, here's shame, here's fear, here's disappointment. I don't want to feel these. I'm going to have a couple of beers and a banana nut muffin. I don't want to feel these." You can't numb those hard feelings without numbing those other affects or emotions. You cannot selectively numb. So, when we numb those, we numb joy, we numb gratitude, we numb happiness and then we are miserable, and we are looking for purpose and meaning and then we feel miserable, so we have a couple of beers and a banana nut muffin. And it becomes this dangerous cycle.[61]

---

61 TEDx talk: The Power of Vulnerability – Brené Brown, June 2010

You can't learn to guard against vulnerability without affecting joy and gratitude and the ability to connect fully. Your emotions are not going to let you abuse them repeatedly without trying to protect themselves. The more you find yourself in situations where you are vulnerable, and you get hurt because it is unsafe, the more likely you will be to avoid being vulnerable in the future. We do not need to avoid vulnerability, ever. We need to avoid being in situations where being vulnerable is imprudent or unwise. We need to avoid situations where it feels safe to be vulnerable and prematurely expose our deeper emotions when those situations are not permanent and are, in fact, not safe. If we learn to guard our situations much more than our emotions so that we never have to learn from the pain of being emotionally injured, how much easier will it be to truly connect on an emotional level when it is safe, and the relationship is genuinely secure?

This is why we can connect with Jesus like no one else. We can be truly vulnerable with Him because he is truly safe. When we are looking to truly connect with someone, Jesus will never disappoint us or hurt us or prove to be unreliable. We never have to be concerned with Jesus breaking our heart, so we can give our hearts fully to Him.

If your heart has already been through the wringer with other dating relationships, or maybe you grew up in an emotionally turbulent or toxic environment, Jesus is the answer. Jesus can completely heal the pain of the deepest wounds, no matter how old the wounds and no matter how deep the wounds. Depending on what happened to you and how it happened, you might still have scar tissue from your past hurts, but the wounds can be fully healed. And the best news is when you are in relationship with Jesus Christ, He will ultimately take away even the scar tissue for all of eternity.

The Problem with Exclusivity

The Heart Trap

I THINK EVERYONE gets crushes from time to time. You see someone new and she's cute and she seems smart and kind and intriguing. Or maybe she's just really good looking. She might be the new girl in class, or she might be the weather woman on the local news. The only things that are true for all crushes is that you know almost nothing at all about this person, and you are interested anyway. Now generally speaking, if the object of your interest is someone who is accessible, he or she would be the person you begin to maneuver around so that you might be able to figure out how you might initiate a relationship. Or if you're anything like me, she is the person who immediately draws your full attention any time you're in the same room and the same person who you can't even look at in the eyes because your heart and brain paralyze with fear. You think if you look at her, she will know you're interested in talking to her and she would be freaked out. So, you may commence being unintentionally but very effectively unfriendly or antisocial towards this person who has probably never had any meaningful interaction with you at all – a bit counterintuitive.

Whether you are the ambitious angler, or you are the painfully shy, establishing this exclusive mental interest and developing a crush is not going to help you get what (or who) you ultimately want. I realize there are varying degrees of natural assertiveness, so it doesn't matter whether you are at either extreme or somewhere in the middle. Isolating or categorizing in your mind as a potential romantic interest someone you barely know or do not know at all is a potentially bad thing for everyone involved. It might not necessarily be harmful, *per se*, but it is not going to do you any favors in the short or long term.

One of the biggest reasons why it is to your detriment that you fixate on one person, despite how worthy you might think he or she is, or even how worthy everyone else says they are, is the other people in the room. If you want a fulfilling, long-lasting, committed marriage relationship at some point in the future, it will be in your best interest to not lose sight of other people in the room; it's a bad idea to treat any one person differently than anyone else if the sole reason for you treating that person differently is infatuation. This means not giving them either more or less attention than you might otherwise to anyone else in the room. There are probably many people around you with whom you might have mutually beneficial, edifying and encouraging interactions. It will be much more difficult for you to sincerely engage with others if most or all of your attention is occupied by just one other person in the room.

Now at some point if it gets to this particular point, your brain may quite literally not allow you to think of this person (and, by extension, treat them) the same way as everyone else. Eventually, if you let it, you will lose the ability to direct your thoughts when that person is present. But at the very first, when the seeds of infatuation have not developed into a full-blown overwhelming crush, you do have full control of the volume and intensity of your thoughts.

The first thing you must do is reign in your thoughts and feelings to not allow your feelings to overdevelop too quickly. In order to control your thoughts, you will have to stop thinking of everyone (or any one person in particular) as potential future mates.

If you spend a good amount of time before being around any particular person thinking about how you might be able to engineer a situation where you can interact, or where you can be noticed by that person, you're probably on the wrong track. If you spend an inordinate amount of time when you're not around that person thinking about that person or reading his or her social media pages, this is a sign you might be a little too far down the road of infatuation. If you are in a situation where you are looking for excuses to text or direct message the person in whom you have discovered this developing interest, you might want to take some time to course-correct. There are other signs as well, anything along the lines of drawing your singular focus because of a potential romantic attraction, should signify that you are allowing your infatuation to spiral.

Society has taught us that this infatuation is okay with only one caveat: you need to eventually make that connection so that you can start dating. Then everything from before is worth it and everything will turn out okay. But, just like a singular focus on a single object of affection is not a good thing before you have established a connection or started actually dating that person, there are terrible effects of that singular focus when you are dating that person as well. This singular focus while dating is what we think of as being exclusive. Exclusivity is a beautifully necessary component of a healthy marriage, but premature exclusivity before you are married comes with some very bad consequences.

Territorialism

Premature exclusivity has all sorts of negative consequences. One of the most common and least redeemable consequences of exclusivity is territorialism. Ladies, I don't know if you know the practice I'm about to describe actually happens, but I will not be surprised if when you hear about it, it frustrates you. I'm not sure if it's purely social pressure and expectation that perpetuate this, but it really needs to stop.

Here is the scenario. A group of Christian guys are hanging out together. One of the guys in the friend circle declares that he is interested in a female that they all know. The moment any guy expresses his interest in a girl to any of his friends, that girl automatically becomes off-limits to all the other guys. I'm not sure why this happens, but it does. Even if there is another guy in the group who also likes the girl, even if that other guy has a lot more interests in common with her, or has a personality that compliments hers perfectly, or has the exact sense of humor that she does, or already spends more time with her, or any number of other valid reasons to want to be able to pursue her – it is only the guy who speaks up about her first and declares his interest in her first that is socially allowed to do anything publicly to express his interest in her. This guy might be the worst fit for her and everyone suspects it, but that doesn't matter. All that matters is he called her first.[62]

This is a well-established and frustratingly real phenomenon. There are several crude but rhyming phrases that exist in our society that describe the brazen pariah who might dare to "get in the way" of another guy who wants to pursue a girl, as well as a similarly crude but rhyming phrase to describe the general ethic of not "getting in the way" of another guy for the sake of a female

---

[62] "Called," as in a manner of reserving something – like with a coin-flip; not as in telecommunicating.

interest. The phrases are dumb. The practice is dumb. The guys who subscribe to this behavior are not doing themselves or anyone else any favors when it comes to being in a long-term, committed, fulfilling relationship. It's still possible to get the relationship you really want; this just make it so much harder.

It actually gets worse/sillier because there is no statute of limitations on a guy being able to reserve a young lady for himself. Even if he drags his feet without asking her out for weeks or months, as long as his interest does not waver, any other guy in the group will respect the claim that he staked and not "get in the way" of the guy with the declared interest. There is one caveat to this rule: if the first guy does take a very long time to attempt any active pursuit and another guy does want to ask this girl out, he may only do so if he gets the first guy's permission! Even if the first guy doesn't drag his feet in expressing interest, but the girl doesn't reciprocate, the rules still apply. Even if the entire group of males knows he has asked her out on a date, and she's made it clear that she is not interested, as long as his interest in her does not waver, no other guy in the friend group is allowed to express interest in her.

This situation can be extremely frustrating to any other guy who thinks he might have interested in the girl. I have been in the position on multiple occasions when the second guy will express to me how he feels trapped between his feelings for a girl and the social rules of his male friend group. I have seen first-hand how one guy who probably would have been much better suited for a particular young lady never got the chance because, while he was trying to be cautious and circumspect, another guy was being less-so and made it known first that he was interested.

So, ladies, this is why it seems like at most one guy at a time is interested in you. Sometimes this is also why it seems like no guys are interested in you. If the first guy is too hesitant or reserved to make a move and his friends don't let you know what's going on, you may never be approached for the sake of the male rules governing that guy's "right" of first refusal for you. Now, how dumb is that? Very dumb. And guys know it's dumb. But they do it anyway! No matter what, this really needs to stop.

Blink Dating

One of the most compelling reasons to not become infatuated with one person, allowing your desire to isolate that person in your thoughts, is that despite what you think right now, you really don't know what you want. The frightening thing is that we can think we are certain about what we want, but we actually don't have a clue. What you are looking for in a person is a very personal thing. You might like someone whose strongest characteristic is being funny, or you might like someone who is funny, but his most prominent characteristic is kindness. There is definitely no right or wrong answer as to what you like in a person.[63] But what if what you think you want in a person changes to something completely different, and then can change back based on your circumstances.

In Malcolm Gladwell's 2005 book *Blink: The Power of Thinking without Thinking*[64], he tells the story of a group of New York City speed daters who are undergoing a social psychology experiment but they are unaware of it. It goes like this: two scientists were trying to figure out if people knew what they were looking for when they were speed dating, so before the evening began, they asked the participants of this speed dating night to rate on a scale of 1 to 10 what they were looking for in a date. The categories

---

63 Because no one likes it when the other person's most obvious trait is being a pathological liar, and no one is going to choose someone because she is quick-tempered or other obviously ugly traits.

64 Gladwell, Malcolm (2005). *Blink: The Power of Thinking Without Thinking*. Back Bay Books, Little, Brown.

the participants had to rate were: attractiveness, shared interests, sense of humor, sincerity, intelligence and ambition. The participants were asked to give their ratings right before the speed dating, then the next day, then again one month later, and then again in six months.

When the scientists looked at the matches each participant made that night, they discovered some fascinating things. What the speed daters say they want beforehand and what they were actually attracted to during the evening didn't match. Then, when the scientists asked the daters the next day to assess what they would look for in a date, the daters' answers would not be what they declared they initially wanted before the speed dating began. Instead, their answers mirrored who they chose the night before. The part that was most fascinating to me is that after a month when asked again, their answers reset back to their pre-speed date answers! This means what you think you want can change almost immediately to something completely different than what you really want if you are under the influence of infatuation.

Gladwell suggests that decisions of who you are attracted to (at least in a speed dating scenario) are usually governed by emotions and impulse, not a thoughtful, measured list. He calls it a story-telling problem. You try to come up with a logical explanation for something that does not have a logical explanation. When we are in a situation when emotions run high, like a situation when we are trying to decide on one person, we are much more likely to ignore or completely forget about logic and lists. Now, I'm not about to suggest that falling in love is a completely logical process, nor should it be, nor does it need to be to get what you really are looking for. What I will say is that you would be better served and much more likely to end up with what you want (with a lot less hassle and heartache) if you can pay a bit more attention to some of the things that our current process makes us much more likely to ignore. Said another way, you will not be able to control your feelings of affection, but you can leverage your circumstances and leverage the process so that those things work entirely in your favor.

The Perils of Comparison

Another set of problems arise because of exclusivity within a dating relationship. Let me state the obvious. If you have not yet proposed marriage or accepted a marriage proposal, then you are still in the evaluation and decision-making phase of your relationship. You might not be actively evaluating the person you're dating, but that does not change the fact that you have not yet fully and finally decided on your mate, 'til death do you part. But while you are deciding, you are only dating one person at a time. We live in a culture of exclusivity. However, exclusivity in this phase creates some unique situations that make it harder for you to find what you are actually looking for.

Inevitably, the longer you spend time dating someone, the more you will find out about that person. You will discover all sorts of character traits, personality traits, his strange interests, hobbies, collections and quirks. You will learn things that you like about him that you didn't know you would end up liking. But eventually, you will begin to discover things that perhaps aren't the best, maybe even things that are annoying. You might even discover things that make compatibility with you a particular challenge, or perhaps, even a "deal-breaker." And as you are in the evaluation stage, this is exactly what you need to be doing – giving an honest evaluation of your compatibility.

There are a couple of problems with this scenario of evaluation: if you are in a committed exclusive relationship, you will probably be tempted to try to make the relationship work. If you have chosen one person on whom you are focusing your romantic attention, the emotional investment you made is going to motivate you focus on your similarities and the things that will lead to positive evaluation. You will be tempted to overlook things that perhaps need not be overlooked for the sake of "giving it a chance" or "making it work." The fact that you have already chosen one person (even though you are still in the choosing stage) and that one person has chosen you (even though they can still change their mind) will make any negative evaluations you need to make harder to see, and then harder to admit to. Let's also not forget about the speed dating lesson.

Beyond the negative things being harder to identify in the person you are dating, if you are looking for areas of incompatibility or areas of concern while you are in a committed relationship you won't actually be giving the relationship its best shot. In other words, unless you are dating a perfect person, if you look long enough and hard enough you will find some things you don't like about the person you're dating. It is going to be a very difficult task for you to wholeheartedly seek to give the relationship you're in its best chance for success if you're looking for reasons that it might not last in the long run. This exclusivity creates a paradox of conundrum. Looking to make it work will almost necessarily mean overlooking some things, but looking to see if the relationship might need to end means looking for things that need not be scrutinized. You will not be able to earnestly and honestly do both at the same time. So, unless you have already made the proper choice, this exclusivity will make things difficult. Even if you have chosen someone who might have been the proper choice otherwise, this situation is baiting you to unnecessarily ruin a relationship that might not need be ruined by searching for and focusing on things that need not be focused on. And perish the thought that you see a reason to end it, but are working so hard on sustaining the relationship that you ignore or justify away red flags all the way through engagement and marriage. Let's not do things that people who end up choosing poorly do.

Exclusivity also makes it harder for you figure out what you're looking for. Remember the speed dating story from *Blink*? The speed daters changed the characteristics they said they wanted based on the people they had already chosen. You might think you want and erudite with dry humor because that's who you are currently dating; so, if you actually would be better off with a down-to-earth goof-ball, the fact that you're with the sardonic academic is likely to distort what you think you actually want. He might pass all your tests, but are you sure you didn't mistakenly exchange your real test for one that matches him perfectly? Or one that will be impossible for him to fail because you have been swept up by him? One of the most annoying things about your own heart is that you can't trust it when you need to most. When your heart is speaking loudly about something emotional, most of the time you can't help but listen to and be persuaded by it. That is problematic.

Ownership

Most of the fundamental problems with exclusivity come from the reality that whereas there are lots of benefits from being in an indefinite, fully-committed relationship that people want to experience through dating, marriage is the only version of that relationship type for which people were designed. The benefits of marriage are only to be enjoyed inside a marriage relationship. Otherwise, there are consequences. Even though sometimes those "consequences" are experienced whether you are married or not, a marriage is designed with those consequences in mind. Any other relationship type, namely, a long-term dating relationship, will suffer because of it. One of the bigger consequences that shows up because of exclusivity in relationship is the idea and the effects of ownership.

I need to be clear and careful about the way I talk about this concept because this is one area where I can be easily (and quickly) misunderstood. When two people get married, the husband doesn't own his wife and the wife doesn't own her husband. It has been illegal to own another human being in North America for some time now. They don't own each other. But, then again, they kind of do.

In one of the most famous passages on marriage in the Bible, the Apostle Paul gives instructions on the relationship between husbands and wives. He says, "Wives, submit to your own husbands, as to the Lord."[65] That phrase "your own husbands" signifies a possession of ownership. The Greek word *idios*[66] means belonging to one's self. Right now, we are talking about why this concept is very dangerous outside of marriage, but inside marriage, this one sentence is the very key to a wonderful, God honoring relationship. It is telling both husbands and wives to intentionally be subject, or submit, to the one who belongs to you. The verse before it says a similar thing, "submitting to one another out of reverence for Christ."[67] Submit your own control to the other. Intentionally let the other person control you. It's the concept of mutual submission. When both the husband and wife get this idea and follow it, each person submitting to and serving the other at any cost is the most beautiful thing.

We are supposed to submit to and serve others, but when we are in an exclusive non-marriage relationship, this duty of service to another gets distorted. We want to honor the wishes of this

---

65 Ephesians 5:22

66 Strong's G2398

67 Ephesians 5:21

other person, a lot of times regardless of the cost, and this is a noble thing on its face. However, a lot of times our motives are distorted and any healthy boundaries we might otherwise have in our pursuit of service are stretched too far or altogether eliminated. People who are in a long-term dating relationship often experience this sense of entitled ownership. There is nothing wrong with experiencing someone else serving you, but there is something wrong with feeling like they owe it to you based on your relationship with them. But we do it.

If your girlfriend ever wanted to go to dinner with another guy without you, would you have a problem with it? If he was a long-time, old friend it might be okay, right? But wouldn't you expect her to invite you along? Or ask if you're okay with it? And if you said you weren't okay with it, wouldn't you expect her to call it off? And if she didn't, wouldn't you be angry? Because there are unwritten rules in dating that she no longer gets to go out with whomever she wants. Maybe coffee is okay, but dinner isn't. Or maybe dinner is even okay, but a wedding escort without you isn't. Or maybe the line is a movie. Somewhere along the line in some context, you are not okay with the person you are dating spending time with someone of the opposite sex in the same way you might be perfectly fine with someone else you're not dating doing the same thing. This is because you feel entitled, at least to some extent, to be able to direct his or her time. When you do this, you're acting like at least a part owner of his or her life. You feel entitled to because you're dating. Now, there are certainly lots of things you can learn when the person you're dating wants to go out on a date with someone else, and you should certainly take heed. The problem is that your relationship does not give you actual authority over any part of his or her time. The right you feel that you have to be upset in situations like this is actually imaginary.

When you have a formal event with your sorority or a friend of yours is getting married or you have an important work function where spouses are invited, do you expect your significant other to go with you? Is he allowed to say, "I'm not doing anything else that evening, but I just don't want to go"? If he has another conflict, that's one thing, but can he just say no? Of course not! Because if it's important to you and you're dating, you feel as if he has to go. Or if he decides not to go and you don't force him to go, you will be upset with him. The reason you feel like you can justifiably be upset in situations like this is because you have a sense of entitlement on the time of the other person. Because you are exclusively dating, you feel as if you have a claim of ownership over his life. Maybe you don't expect him to spend every moment with you – but you expect he will some of the time. Maybe you even enjoy your space when he's hanging out with the fellas away from you, but you know, and he knows, he is not allowed to hang out with the ladies away from you.

As we know it, and as we understand it; what I just described is perfectly okay. It's the way that everyone operates. I mean, most people don't call it "ownership" because that sounds pretty controlling and dehumanizing and even illegal, but the general idea is widely accepted and even expected. But whether you want to have it or not, a dating relationship does not come along with the right to have any part of another belong to you. Societal expectation and personal attempts to please the person you're dating are the only forces by which this idea exists in a dating relationship. The stress that someone else exhibiting measures of ownership upon you puts on your relationship with that person can severely damage the relationship. This strain will show up whenever you don't want to do the thing they want you to do, or when the person you're dating is not cooperating with something that means so much to you. *It's just one art gallery opening and I need you to want to be there with me.* Or *why would you even want to spend time with another girl?* Situations like these that are big enough or that happen frequently enough can lead directly to a breakup. There is only one relationship whose very design is built to withstand the expectations and constraints of ownership and submission to another person, and that relationship is not the dating relationship. It's marriage.

The Breakup

When you enter an exclusive dating relationship with someone, that relationship can end in only two ways: breakup or marriage. Those are your only two options. Even if a breakup is not particularly difficult, it's still a breakup. Also, and I'm not going to harp on this at all, but just because a breakup was not very difficult for you, doesn't mean the breakup was not very difficult.

Breakups are painful. They are supposed to be. Something with potential has ended. Something you invested in has died. You put time, energy, emotion, care, creativity and so many other valuable things into a relationship, and regardless of why it ended, it hurts to end. Almost always when you enter a relationship with someone, you know that a breakup is possible, but you never really think the breakup will be inevitable.

Culture will tell you that breakups are unavoidable. And if you date the only way that culture has taught us to date, culture is almost totally right. There are two ways within the normal bounds of culture to avoid a breakup: marry the first person you date or never date at all. For someone who wants to get married, neither of these are ideal options. Even though it *can* happen that you might end up marrying the first person you ever date, it's pretty unlikely.[68] It goes without saying that choosing marriage solely to avoid a breakup is one of the worst reasons anyone could possibly have to get married.

---

68 Please don't put that kind of pressure on yourself or someone else by expecting to marry the first person you ever date. That expectation is not good for anyone.

Usually, the longer you date someone exclusively, the more complicated the breakup, the more difficult the breakup, and the longer and more painful the relationship recovery process ends up being. The only good thing about a breakup is that you are no longer attached to someone with whom, as time has revealed, you are better off not being attached. But even this very good news is not much conciliation in the midst of a breakup and sometimes does not reveal itself to be true until much later. To say nothing of the occasions when that truth never reveals itself because the person you broke up with (for whatever reason the breakup occurred) really was awesome and your regret will never totally disappear. The best you can hope for in this situation is that you won't think very often for the rest of your life of what could have been. Thankfully, this situation is usually only imaginary and fades away as quickly as the pain of the breakup dissipates.

There is another nefarious thing that breakups do. They help us practice for divorce when we do get married. I'm not saying that breakups and divorce are the same thing. They're not. I'm not going to pretend I have a clue of the magnitude of devastation and pain people go through should they have to go through a divorce. I'm not going to compare divorce and breakups in the same way I contrast marriage and dating. But the way that people think about relationships as an entity with a beginning and ending, the way that we do assess the person we are dating and look for reasons to end it, the way that we practice tolerating the person we are with only to the point we realize they are not worth the trouble, and yes, the way we learn to navigate the heartache and pain we experience after the relationship ends, help shape a culture where the temporary nature of commitment in relationship is normal. When we become accustomed to ending relationships before marriage, what exactly do we think is different about marriage that will negate what we've been practicing all along?

The Problem with Commitment

THE IDEA OF commitment in relationship is really the hinge point in thinking clearly about contemporary society's concept of healthy dating. The idea of commitment is probably the thing that bothers me most about the way people try to date. Commitment is one of the most important aspects of a healthy romantic relationship. It is also the thing that we have the most incorrect view about. If you want to walk down the road of relationships in a way that does not make what you're trying to do harder for yourself, you need to understand what commitment is, what it isn't, and where it actually exists.

As we've said before and as you already know, when two people are dating, they remain boyfriend and girlfriend until they either get married or break up. When you are dating someone, you can decide to end that relationship at any time for any reason, or for no reason at all. We need to slow down and think about that last sentence. People who are dating, no matter how long they've been dating can break up any time they want to. They might have a really good reason. They might have a really awful reason. They might have no reason at all. It might make perfect sense and be long overdue. It might be impulsive and make no sense. The decision to break up does not have to be logical or mutual. It's also not always predictable. When you are in a dating relationship, there is no real guarantee that the relationship will last past tomorrow, regardless of how strongly you feel about it today.

Merriam-Webster defines commitment as an agreement or pledge to do something in the future.[69] This definition helps to more clearly reveal the biggest problem with commitment in a dating relationship. This biggest problem is that commitment in a dating relationship is not real. It might feel real, but it's not. You might behave like the commitment is real, but it's not real. If you don't hear anything else in this entire book (besides the fact that Jesus came so that you can be reconciled to God) please hear this. This one fact should compel you to entirely change the way you think about dating and relationships. This one fact should make you desperate to know a better way to engage in a romantic relationship without having to base your strategies and behaviors on a falsehood. Here it is. If you have the freedom to end your dating relationship at any time for any reason, and commitment has to do with a pledge for future behavior, dating relationships **do not involve a real commitment with the person you are dating.** For the rest of this chapter, my only goal is to make sure you are clear about this. If you aren't convinced yet, I'm going to take some time to try and convince you by pointing out things you probably already know but have never taken the time to admit to yourself. I am going to try to convince you to want to change your thoughts on dating as we know it and your corresponding behaviors because this is so very important. At the very least, I want to stop you from being naive. If you decide to continue acting like dating is something it is not, you will not be able to say, "I didn't know. Nobody ever told me." Because I'm telling you now.

---

69 Merriam-Webster, Commitment

False Sense of Security

The most obvious problem with acting like dating relationships establish commitment is there is a false sense of security. Real security can be found in relationships that are founded on true commitment. It's one of the many amazing gifts that can be found inside the true commitment of marriage. Dating, however, does not have the same real security of marriage. Just as a reminder, the relationship can end at *any time* for *any reason*. There is zero security in that.

There is surely some part of you that realized that there is no true security in a dating relationship. The younger you are and the shorter the duration of the relationship, the easier this is to see. If you are still living at home and your parents are still paying for most of your life, chances are it is your parents who are the primary providers of your financial, emotional, and relational security. Whether you realize it or not, your parents will probably be a huge buffer in any relational mistakes you make. For those of you who have moved out or have begun the trek to independence from your parents (having moved out does not automatically mean you have moved any closer to independence, but it can be an indicator), you won't have as much of a benefit of having your parents being a built-in stability force for the storms of your life.

Even though you might know doing so is not the wisest course of action, the longer you date someone, the more you start to intertwine your life with your significant other's life. It's what we think we're supposed to do based on the teachings of society. In fact, society will tell you that if you're not finding security in the person you're dating, your relationship might not be working the way it is supposed to be working. This is one of the places where the degree to which you are exclusive will make the effects of the misplaced security much worse. People who are dating will not only start to add their boyfriend or girlfriend to the routine, but they will start to rely on them in the same way they rely on their car to take them to work.[70] Do you feel like you have to text your boyfriend or girlfriend as soon as you wake up in the morning? Have you become accustomed to your boyfriend or girlfriend being the last call or text of your day? Do you primarily or solely use your him or her as the person you turn to when you are having a bad day? Or when you have reason to celebrate? Or when you are feeling sad or otherwise emotional? Is your boyfriend or girlfriend in on all your inside jokes?

Relying on the person you are dating is using them as sort of balance for your life. You may be relying on the person you are dating to tell you when you're being too weird, or too timid, or too stubborn. You may start to think that all your happy moments would be happier if he or she were here to experience them with you – all your sad moments would be more bearable too. And if he or she is not there, they're the first person you tell about it when you get the chance. You may feel you can always count on him or her to pick you up when you're feeling down. Ultimately, you would readily admit that he or she is your best friend. Society would tell you that this is the picture of health in relationship. And they are totally right in that declaration as long as the relationship is one that is founded in true commitment. But if your relationship is not based on true commitment, if the person you are with could decide to end the relationship tomorrow for any reason (without violating any of God's commands simply based on the act of that decision), then looking to that other person for security is foolish. And by the way, most of my examples were about relational and emotional security, but financial security, or physical security, or spiritual security, or any other type of security is just as foolish and dangerous.

I want to say one more thing before I move on. This desire for

---

70 Or if you take the bus or ride the subway or slide down a fire pole, my point of relying on something inside of a routine remains.

security you have is a good thing. You have it because God gave it to you. It is natural, and it's supposed to be filled. It's just not supposed to be filled by a boyfriend or a girlfriend. If you're being honest and your boyfriend or girlfriend is serving that purpose in your life, they are not enough to make you feel truly secure. And what do you do if the person you turn to when you need to feel better is the reason you're upset?

Maintenance not Evaluation

Another negative effect of false commitment in a dating relation-ship is what it does inside of the relationship. If you are dating, it means you are not engaged or married. If you are not yet engaged or married, it means that you are still in the decision-making phase. By the way, if you are a male and you have already decided that she is the one, why are you not engaged yet?[71] When you are in a dating relationship, you have decided on one person; but you have yet to decide whether you want to be with that person to the extent that you want to fully commit for the rest of your life. Because of the idea of false commitment, you are going to be much less likely to objectively determine if this person is right for you. Instead, you are going to be inclined to try to make the relationship work. You may choose to maintain the status of your relationship, as opposed to evaluating with ending the relationship in mind.

One of the other dangerous ideas that society attaches to breakups is characterizing them as a failure of your relationship. Since most people don't want anything they are a part of to fail, your impulse will most certainly be to not allow the relationship to fail unless it really has to. Now, in any relationship with another human who is flawed, there are going to be some things about the

---

71 If you have a good reason, you should contact me and let me know what it is. I bet the reason is not as good as you think it is. Let's discuss.

73

other person that you will not like and you will have to learn to accept; however, it is easier to properly determine if these negative things need to be accepted, or if they serve as a signals to end the romance, if you are not prematurely predisposed to avoid relationship failure based on the fact that you made a commitment to date the person you are dating.

Pressure

The false commitment of the dating relationship has another perilous inherent flaw that can often rear its ugly head: pressure. Whether you have admitted it out loud to yourself in clear and unmistakable terms or not, the fact that your boyfriend or girlfriend can in fact decide to end the relationship at any time for any reason is not lost on most people. So, this means that if you are not ready to end the relationship, you will feel pressure to make sure the person you're dating wants to remain in the relationship too. After all, no one wants to be dumped. Getting into a real relationship is so hard in the first place because trying to find someone who is potentially suitable is not very fun for most people and usually comes with a certain amount of stress. Therefore, if you get past those initial hurdles to the point where you have committed to being in a relationship, the rational thing to do is try your hardest to remain in the relationship. Like we talked about in the last section, part of you trying to remain in the relationship is possibly ignoring things you would be better served to not ignore. A consequence of trying to keep the relationship alive is the way you will feel pressured to change yourself.

A couple of years ago, as I was preparing to give the relationships talk that was the catalyst for this book, I had the honor of visiting a few times with a marriage counselor who helped me work through many of my ideas. One of the things he discussed with me was the idea of people who were dating putting on a facade. You feel pressure, which is usually (but not always) self-generated to change yourself to be the person you think the person you're with wants to be with. Essentially, you pretend to be a slightly different version of yourself because you think you'll have a better chance of sustaining the relationship. Or think of it as sacrificing certain aspects of yourself for the other person. It could be subconscious changes you might not even realize. Or maybe you are fully aware that you are a jerk or a basket case and you're just trying to fake it as long as you can to see how far you can develop the relationship.

In one of the conversations I had with the marriage counselor, he told me that he had counseled a couple who had been married for nine months before they took their masks off and learned to stop faking who they actually were to each other. What a scary thought. If the person you're dating is doing this to keep you in the relationship, you might literally have no idea who you are dating or, eventually, literally not know the person who you might end up actually marrying. Maybe they are wearing the mask on purpose or don't even realize they are doing it, but the pressure of a commitment which they know can be as temporary as any time and any reason, and the fear of losing a person or a relationship they don't want to lose, is sufficient motivation for them to put on the facade. You might not be dating someone who does this, and you might not do this yourself, but it does not change the fact that it is a reality that comes with the way dating exists in our society.

Less Freedom

I know I'm piling it on, but I want to make certain that you are not only aware of the many problems that come with the commitment of a dating relationship, but that you will no longer settle for this unnecessarily complex and difficult method of trying to find a spouse. If you're already convinced, you can just go ahead and skip to the next chapter. If not, let us continue. I have a friend who was dating this girl one fall and they had been dating for over a year. Like most people who have been exclusively dating for that long, he would say that he was in a committed relationship with her. His younger brother was a starting wide receiver on the high school football team, and his brother's team was in the playoffs with a game one Friday night. That same night, our church was hosting its annual international Thanksgiving dinner where international students from over 50 countries come to celebrate a Thanksgiving meal and interact with table hosts who are volunteers from our church congregation. There are two table hosts for each table, and lots of times couples will sign up to serve together at a table. You can see where this is going.

My friend wanted to go to his brother's game and his girlfriend wanted to serve international students in an environment where they might hear the gospel for the first and maybe only time. Now the option of them deciding to just do separate activities is obvious for something like this situation, and it's also something that they discussed, but the way that the two of them interpreted their commitment to one another did not allow them to make that obvious choice. Further, even if they had decided to do separate things that night, the choice would have come with negative feelings. For the sake of the integrity of the relationship and his commitment to his girlfriend, the guy did not feel the freedom to go to his brother's game. He did not have a commitment to the Thanksgiving banquet, but he did feel like he had a commitment to his girlfriend. She wanted him to be with her that night, and he didn't want to disappoint her. He wanted to serve her and demonstrate his commitment to her by choosing to do something that was important to her.

You probably have been in a similar situation or know friends who have been. It's one thing if you want to sacrifice your desires for a boyfriend or a girlfriend, and that type of sacrifice is commendable indeed. But sometimes you will feel trapped in a decision you don't want to make. Sometimes you want to make that selfless decision, but sometimes you can feel cornered by the commitment you made to the relationship.[72]

Isolation from Community

It's easy for us to feel like we have more to lose in our dating relationships than any other type of relationship we are in, so we want to take enough time and care to cultivate it. We might feel more comfortable with our boyfriend or girlfriend than with anyone else. Eventually, it becomes easier to be with them than with anyone else. Ironically, even if you end up fighting all the time, even the fighting becomes familiar and we are comfortable and familiar with comfortable. We will start to choose this relationship over other relationships. We will also be tempted to spend more time alone with the person we are dating than is good for a truly balanced and healthy relationship. There will be times when you spend time with your significant other instead of spending time with other same-sex relationships with whom you are in community, and there is nothing necessarily wrong with doing this, but you will be more and more likely to choose your significant other over your friends.

You will be more likely to request time of your boyfriend or girlfriend that he or she might have spent developing other relationships in community. Your time is a scarce and valuable resource and deciding how to spend it will always be a challenge to do well. The big problem is that the commitment of a dating relationship will influence the way you spend your time in a way that counter-intuitively makes it more difficult to find yourself in a healthy, lasting, long-term relationship. This heightened commitment to this other person causes you to spend too much time

---

72 His brother's team ended up winning the game that night, in case you were wondering.

alone together and not enough time with other relationships that could actually serve your romantic relationship better if those other varied relationships are developed to the point where they can help. And as with everything else, you can still find the relationship you're looking for through this type of isolation, but it will be much more difficult than it has to be. Don't make yourself walk uphill if you don't have to.

Sexual Compromise

All the alone time – the fact that he or she is so special to you and you want to express your feelings. The fact that she is really good looking. The fact that society tells you you're supposed to, though you don't need society to prompt you for this one; but society surely isn't doing anything to stop you. The longer you date, because you feel like you're committed, because you feel like you're safe with the person, because you feel comfortable, more and more. Because you want to. You will be much more likely to find yourself in situations where you compromise your sexual boundaries, regardless of where you set them for yourself.

Your desire for physical intimacy is God-given and there is absolutely nothing wrong with having that desire. What is going to get in the way of you getting what you really want in a relationship is when you decide for yourself to express your intimacy in the ways generally endorsed by society. The longer you are with the person you are dating, the easier it will be for you to compromise yourself sexually, either accidentally or intentionally. The longer you are with him or her, the more you will want to make that compromise. And if you begin to do it, you need to know that your sexuality is an appetite. You will want more and more in order to satisfy yourself, but you will never be fully satisfied. All of this is fueled and protected by the idea of safety that comes with your commitment. If what you really want is a healthy, intimate, long-term, fulfilling romantic relationship, you probably would not rationally break your sexual boundaries with someone who you know won't stick around even until tomorrow because there is no safety with someone who will be gone tomorrow.

The harsh reality is that if you are not engaged or married, the person you're with can choose to end the relationship at any time for any reason. Rationally speaking, there is as much guarantee in that relationship as in one where you just met that day. The most dangerous difference is you have every incentive to treat your dating relationship as if the commitment is real. All the time you spent together is real, but your commitment is not real. Please do not operate as if it were real because commitment in dating is not real.

Last Clarification

Hiestand and Thomas talk about this topic well, so I want to refer you to their book *Sex, Dating, and Relationships: A Fresh Approach*; they say the reason why we feel like we have a true commitment is because of shared attraction.[73] If you like only him today and he likes only you today, it feels like you have a true commitment today. The problem is that feeling of attraction has exactly zero bearing on the way you will feel about each other tomorrow. You might have the best intentions for staying together and so might your boyfriend or girlfriend, but the best laid plans of mice and men often go awry.[74] If this feeling were truly enough to constitute a true commitment, nobody would ever break up. Please do not confuse mutual attraction or anything else for a real commitment. That commitment only comes at an engagement that leads to marriage.

---

73 Hiestand, Gerald and Thomas, Jay S. (2012). *Sex, Dating, and Relationships: A Fresh Approach*, Crossway.

74 From "To a Mouse," by Robert Burns

The Problem with Flirting

PEOPLE USE FLIRTING all the time to signify interest or establish rapport with the person or people with whom they are interested in possibly having a dating relationship. Some people flirt because they think flirting is playful and fun. We are about to discuss why flirting is always a bad idea and how flirting makes getting what you actually want more difficult to get in the long run.

What is flirting anyways?

Let's not forget that definitions are so important when we are talking about anything in the realm of dating and relationships. People will use the same words whose meanings are close enough so that what's being said makes perfect sense, but not precisely enough so that there is a true understanding of what is being communicated. The word *flirting* is one of the primary culprits. Clear understanding is of the utmost importance for us, so I will start in the dictionary.

The definition we are going to use is from Merriam-Webster.[75]

---

75 I flirted with the idea of making a joke here about how I was going to use a definition out of a Bible concordance, but flirting is another word that is not

Definition: flirt

Function: intransitive verb

1. to move erratically : *flit* · butterflies flirting among the flowers

2. a : to behave amorously without serious intent · He flirts with every attractive woman he meets.

   b : to show superficial or casual interest or liking · flirted with the idea; also : *experiment* · a novelist flirting with poetry

3. to come close to reaching or experiencing something — used with *with* · flirting with disaster

Function: transitive verb

1. *flick* · They flirt water at each other's faces.

2. to move in a jerky manner · a bird flirting its tail

In the realm of dating and relationships, the second definition of the word will be most useful to us, specifically the first part of that second definition (2a). Flirting here is defined as behaving "amorously without serious intent." The easiest way to justify not using the second part of definition (2b) is to say it's too broad. If you meet anyone for the first time and you demonstrate a casual interest in them, which I would imagine happens often for anyone who is winsome or polite or both, then any initial conversation with someone who is not immediately boring or uninteresting

---

found in the Bible and there is no need to be potentially misleading; plus, I probably shouldn't be so playful about this topic.

could be categorized as flirting. I don't think so. So then, we shall stick with definition 2a.

We are not quite yet finished with the dictionary. To understand what we mean by flirting in definition 2a, we need to be on the same page about the word *amorous*.

Definition: amorous

Function: adjective

1.   strongly moved by love and especially sexual love · amorous couples

2.   being in love : *enamored* – usually used with of · amorous of the girl

3.   a : indicative of love · received amorous glances from her partner

   b : of or relating to love · an amorous novel

We will use definition 1, "strongly moved by love and especially sexual love," to understand the word amorous. And just to be clear, when we are talking about love in this context, we are going to talk about the type of love that the Greeks would call *eros*.[76]

Behaving Amorously Without being Serious

When we put it all together, we get flirting. It's the guy or girl who intentionally behaves in a way with the express purpose of gaining romantic attention or interest from someone of the opposite sex with whom he or she is not engaged or married. Flirting can be done in any number of ways; anything from batting your eyes (with a specific intent) to buying flowers (with a specific intent) to

---

76 Romantic love

particular "friendly" banter (with specific intent). In order for it to be flirting, there must be both action and intent.[77] You cannot accidentally flirt. If you don't know you're flirting (meaning, if you are acting without the intent to behave amorously), then you are not flirting. So, no need to stop blinking any time you're around someone of the opposite sex to be on the safe side to avoid inadvertently flirting with someone. You have to mean to do it to do it.

So, what's the problem with flirting? How else are you supposed to let someone of the opposite sex know that you're interested in them, after all? In fact, I've heard a wise man who I respect very much say in a Sunday school church seminar that young women sometimes "need to rustle the leaves," so to speak, to get a young man's attention. I will say again that you don't have to do what I suggest here. That man's wisdom is something to consider for sure. I'm just convinced that whereas his suggestion might be a good way to get what you think you want, or what you think God wants for you, what I'm about to suggest is a better way to get what you really want without accidentally making things more difficult for yourself.

It is true that if a man never notices any woman, he will be much less likely to get married; and it is also true that if a woman never gets noticed by any man, she will be much less likely to get married. In the contemporary millennial Christian culture, noticing and being noticed is a crucial part of finding the person who you might marry so it must be done. What's important to know is that the way the noticing takes place can matter very much. We will talk later about how a man can best go about noticing women, but for now we are going to talk about one of the most popular ways today: flirting.

Song of Solomon 2:7 says, "I adjure you, O daughters of

---

77 In the legal world, they call these things *actus reus* and *mens rea*

Jerusalem, by the gazelles or the does of the field, that you not stir up or awaken love until it pleases." What exactly does behaving amorously do if not stir up love? By its very definition, the only thing that "behaving amorously" does is stir up or awaken love. And yet we read in God's word to not "awaken love until it pleases."

As defined, flirting is an act done "without serious intent." When love has so pleased, it's okay to stir up and awaken love. Until that point comes, don't stir! Don't awaken! Some people use flirting as a means of establishing or signifying, in essence – awakening, an attraction to another person. If two people are at the point in their relationship where the attraction has not already been formally recognized, do you think love is then ready to be stirred or awakened? Even after being formally recognized, if two people are still near to the very beginning of their relationship, do you think love is then ready to be stirred or awakened?

How many relationships have you been in or heard of where its downfall, or at least an initial problem is moving too fast too soon? The method of establishing a relationship sets the tone for the relationship, at least for a while. Flirting is a method or device to heat the coals of love. The heat of the relationship is a primary determinant of the speed of the relationship. Is it reasonable to think you can superficially heat the coals of love at the very beginning and not have the impulse to move quickly?

And as far as adjusting the tone and speed of a relationship, is it ever a good sign that you need to slow down? If you need to slow down, that means you were going too fast in the first place. If you find yourself needing to slow down, it means you were probably being hasty or impatient. A healthy romantic relationship should never want or need to cool off or slow down. A healthy romance does not backtrack. It should only intensify, even if it is only very slowly. A healthy romance involves patience and a slow, controlled development.

But some of you ladies may say, "The guys around me are clueless (or at least the one guy who I want to express interest in me is). I need to flirt with him to get his attention." This is faulty. Ladies, you do not want to end up with a guy that requires you socially engineering or manipulating the situation for him to begin pursuing you. You are eventually going to want to be with a man who takes the initiative and is assertive. If he is not taking the initiative of his own accord, you might be better served to see this as a missing character trait that makes him either unready or ineligible for your affections. Fight the impulse to accidentally (or intentionally) encourage any man to be passive. He needs to be assertive and pick you. And ladies, you need to pick only one man, not one man at a time; choose not at the beginning of the relationship, but only at the point when you never want to choose another one again.

Women, what you want is a man who will take full initiative. What you want is a man who will engage with you completely of his own accord. If a man you know doesn't know how to do this, tell him to read this book because I'll be covering how to pursue a woman a few chapters from now.

The Flirty Guy

A man who has decided to reject being passive must take the responsibility to express his interest in a female. That expression of interest needs to be sincere. You want to exist in a culture and a social sphere where women can trust that your kindness is simply for the sake of edifying kindness and nothing more. You want to exist in a culture where you get the benefit of the doubt when you do nice things for women, that you aren't angling for anything in return. You want to live in a world where your kindness isn't interpreted to mean something other than it appears, and you get to play a huge role in shaping your environment to be that way. Tell her that you're interested in her first. Then begin showing it, not the other way around.

Men, do not express interest with your actions if you haven't done so clearly with your words. It is negligent of you to do things that prime her heart to be won, if you are not ready to take responsibility for that heart in a marriage. You might think it's fun to pick up or seduce a woman because the inevitable reciprocation of affection, or the physical affection you might get out of it is appealing. But those behaviors are selfish, plain and simple. Those behaviors are harmful to her whether you realize it or not. Her Heavenly Father does not appreciate you mistreating His daughter in such a way, whether you realize it or not. Intentionally trying to win the heart and affections of someone before you have made certain you want to take responsibility for her heart and affections is irresponsible and disrespectful. Please don't do it. Please do not be unkind. It is unkind to demonstrate an insincere or inappropriate affection towards a woman. The same thing applies to you too, ladies.

Ladies, you need to be able to tell the difference between kind and flirty. Don't assume a gesture means something other than what it appears to mean. Learn to give the benefit of the doubt that he is simply being kind. But also, don't be naive. If you think a note or a gesture or a gift (or anything done by a guy who has not clearly communicated his intent beforehand) might be an amorous gesture (remember this speaks to what he actually intends – flirting isn't accidental), ask him directly. You can even ask him before you check with your friends to see if you are reading too much into things. In the same way that you appreciate direct communication, so does he.

If there is confusion between what he is (or what he is not) saying and the way he is behaving, give him the benefit of the doubt by asking him about it. You can say something like, "Jason, can I talk to you for a minute? When you gave me that dozen red roses on Valentine's Day, it made me feel like you were attempting to express romantic interest in me. Since you haven't told me that you are attempting romantic interest in me, how should I properly interpret this gesture?" If you think you are receiving mixed signals, just ask a clear question about the confusion. And to truly honor him as you do it, ask him about it first, before you discuss and analyze the confusion with your friends.

Also, you need to avoid interacting with someone of the opposite sex who you have just met solely for the sake of getting in a romantic relationship with him or her, or to simply not eliminate the possibility of a future relationship. When you are friends in Christian community, you need to interact with him or her for the for the sake of friendship and for the love of Christ. As friends you can learn about each other – her likes and dislikes, and yours, as well as any inherent incompatibilities, *etc.* You develop the relationship without pressure. As friends, you see that person how she really is, not just how she wants you to see her. True friendships are sincere and honest. True friendship doesn't try to hide one's faults. True friendships are warm and comfortable. Warmth does not burn when you get closer. Warmth does not scar when you separate.

You don't flirt with your friends because friends are not amorous with each other. Flirting with someone with whom you are not amorous and with whom you don't have the express intention to be amorous is dishonoring to the other person and it is dishonoring to the relationship. It is misleading to give off signals to another that are not carefully considered. It's selfish because ultimately, you are acting out of your own self-interest. It's disrespectful because the other person deserves to be treated with more consideration.

Nouns and Verbs and Dating

THE MODERN IDEA of dating (and the even more modern ideas of hooking up and one-night stands) hasn't always been the norm for society. Dating has augmented and changed through the years. Obviously if we go back in time far enough, the concept of dating would not exist at all in the way we talk about dating because there was a change in the way we think about dating. But we can even see drastic changes in recent generations.

It all goes back to nouns and verbs. Everything always comes back to nouns and verbs. Back when our parents were of marrying age, a date was a verb. A date was an activity, it was an event, something you did. You would go to a movie. You would go to the local diner or go play putt putt golf. Date was a verb and *dating* was a gerund.[78] But somewhere along the way, that changed.

Somewhere along the way, dating stopped being a verb and it turned into an *identity status*. In today's society, if you are dating, you are defining who you are in terms of another person. When someone says, "We are dating," she says it to describe the state of existence of a relationship with another person. Dating is now

---

78 Merriam-Webster says a gerund is an English noun formed from a verb by adding *-ing*

no longer a gerund. Dating is a thing. It's a noun. And not only a noun – it has become its own category of relationship.

We use the term "dating" to distinguish romantic relationships from non-romantic relationships. You might go and have coffee with a friend of yours. You might have lunch with the same person every week. But unless you have agreed[79] to enter into a relationship with that person, you would never declare that you are dating them. Furthermore, and this one is really tricky and confusing, even if you go out on a prearranged social engagement with a single member of the opposite sex, unless you have expressed some sort of romantic intent, you're probably not going to call this thing a date. Even if you do call it a date, you wouldn't say you're dating that person after just one date or even two dates. Recently, people have begun calling going on a single date with someone with whom you haven't expressed any direct interest "hanging out." As if not calling it a date will make it not a date....

My point is that the words date and dating can mean something in this era that they didn't mean in eras past. Strangely enough though, those words still have their old meanings as well even in modern society. We all just know to carefully pay attention to context and the implied intent of the speaker when we hear those words. Otherwise, madness and confusion may ensue. If multiple dates is dating, then you can be dating someone you are not yet dating. So confusing.

There are only three God-ordained categories of relationships in the Bible. Each of these categories have specific rules about sexuality given by God to govern the relationship. The first is the family relationship. This relationship consists of parents and children, brothers and sisters. Sexual relations are prohibited among family members. The second God-ordained relationship is marriage of

---

79 Agreement can be express or tacit – based on the way that relationships are easily confusing and can morph without one or both people realizing it.

husbands and wives. Sexual relations between husband and wife are biblically commanded. The final God-ordained category of relationship consists of everyone else who is not a blood-relative or a spouse. For the sake of discussion and to maintain consistency with other people who have used this framework, we will refer to this category as the neighbor relationship. Sexual relations are prohibited in the neighbor relationship.

Here is the crux of the matter: the concept of dating does not appear expressly in the Bible. In fact, the relationship status of dating does not exist anywhere in the Bible. Dating is a category of relationship that we acknowledge in modern society as a viable one. It's a category we invented. It's a category that we take for granted as one we are supposed to have access to should the situation arise. It's a category of relationship to which we have given value. It's a category that so many people want to be in. It's a category that I am convinced isn't supposed to exist. And yet it does.

We have placed this category we invented somewhere between the God-ordained categories of neighbors and marriage. Dating used to be something they did (bowling) and is now something they are (boyfriend & girlfriend) – a contrived category.

Everyone in our society acknowledges the dating category as real, and most people think of it as valuable. And for the sake of clarity, I would say that fundamentally, the idea of Christian "courting" is exactly the same thing, just with some more specific Christian rules. Just know that when I refer to one, I'm referring to both, and both are making finding a spouse harder. Without fully thinking about what we were doing or the implications of it, we think of dating/courting as a relationship with the same authenticity, legitimacy and validity we give the God-ordained categories of relationships between humans found in the Bible. This is a mistake.

Since we have invented our own category of male/female

relationship, we are forced to invent our own purity guidelines for that category. Can you kiss him or her on the first date? Some well-meaning Christians say sure. Some well-meaning Christians say absolutely not. Some well-meaning Christians don't answer the question by saying don't focus on that. A friend of mine who is a leader of a sports-themed Christian ministry says, "I would never say don't ever kiss because I like kissing." This friend, by the way, is happily married with two kids so her opinion has the validity of experience anchoring it. Some reasonable people might disagree with her, but some reasonable people can also agree with her for some of the same or different reasons.

In their Christian dating book, *Real Men Don't Text*, Ruthie and Michael Dean say about purity guidelines, "The goal of saving sex for marriage is not to shackle your freedom, but to prepare you for a greater future. I don't want to give you a set of guidelines[80] or rules, because you need to *make these decisions for yourself*. But it is very important that you have *specific* boundaries, because in my experience vague boundaries lead to specific regrets."[81] Did you catch that? *I'm not going to give you rules because you need to make your own rules.* So many Christian dating books give this same type of advice to their readers. If premarital sex is as detrimental as I have been saying, this advice is like handing a sharp knife with a blade cover to a five-year old and telling him to go outside and play. The thing is, though, if you take the time to see it, we should not make our own rules because God already has.

---

80 The guidelines that he doesn't want to give are in the next paragraph "The two biggest boundaries we had for our physical relationship were (1) no sleepovers and (2) no kissing lying down. We stopped "making out" six months before our wedding because the temptation was growing stronger, and we wanted to save it all for our wedding night."

81 Dean, Michael and Ruthie (2013). *Real Men Don't Text*, Tynedale, page 60-61

In his book, *What Women Wish You Knew About Dating*,[82] Dr. Stephen W. Simpson talks about the subject of kissing. His book, in my opinion, is by far one of the better books on Christian dating I have ever come across. Dr. Simpson says,

> Much has been said about the trouble kissing can cause. What we don't talk about is why kissing is good. I'm going to encourage you to think differently about kissing. Kissing isn't just "okay" in dating, it's important. Even necessary. I believe that God wants you to kiss your girlfriend. In fact, I believe he thinks it's silly and a bit sad if you don't.

> Kissing is symbolic. It's not always a wanton sexual act resulting from a lack of self-control. When you kiss a woman, you're expressing your feelings in a concrete way. You're showing her that you care about her, that she's special, that you feel a connection with her that you feel with no one else. It's an explicit, unmistakable expression of affection. You put your lips to hers and show her that she means so much to you that you want to express it through physical intimacy. It's not sex. It's not the type of physical intimacy reserved for marriage. But it is a way to express something too dear for words to the woman you care about.

Dr. Simpson then goes on to say that there are some people who disagree with him, and that kissing is more sacred than that. So, there is obviously room for opinions in the matter. Generally, the person you are going to think is right is the one you agree with most. Essentially, you are deciding for yourself what is best

82 Simpson, Stephen (2008). *What Women Wish You Knew About Dating*, Baker Books, page 157

for you, or what is right for you, and you are using other people's opinions and reasoning as your justification.[83]

I don't want to only pick on kissing. What if you spend all your time caressing each other but your lips don't ever lock? Is this any better? Depending on who you talk to, the answer to that question is "Yes," or "No," or "It's up to you whether that is acceptable or not," or even asking, "What did the two of you decide on before the heat of the moment, before you began to express physical expressions of care," or "What did you discuss with your accountability partners?" Christians who do talk about this sort of thing focus on kissing as opposed to things that might be deemed more intimate than kissing for lots of really good reasons, and virtually all[84] of them are arbitrary.

This is why we get to ask the question, "How far is too far?" Since God doesn't tell us how to treat sexuality in this category, and we will necessarily have to treat sexuality some way, someone is going to make the rules for sexuality in a dating relationship. And no one really knows who makes those rules.

A lot of times setting the rules for acceptable sexuality in a dating/courting relationship is a societal or culturally guided agreement. Sometimes it's the parents of the participants who give the rules to the participants (like in courting – though I would imagine those parents would get guidance from the Bible). Sometimes it's a pastor or a youth leader who sets the rule of sexuality to their

---

83 The irony of me speaking into this topic is not lost on me either. I don't think my opinions are truer or more right than anyone else's thoughts on the topic. I just think the way we talk about it in this book will be much more likely to get you what you actually want in the long run without all the negatives that come with other ways of operating, which are just as valid in at least some people's opinions.

84 Even the non-arbitrary statements prohibiting acts short of intercourse based on Ephesians 5:3 and similar verses are arbitrary because there is no definitive list as to what counts as "sexual immorality."

congregations or youth groups, or they at least give guidelines – hopefully with guidance from the Bible.[85] Sometimes it is the two people in the relationship themselves who set the rules based on a mutual agreement of comfort, or what their friends are doing, or what they think would be acceptable. And sometimes the rules are not set at all, which is actually a set of rules as well.

Monogamy has still maintained itself as a virtuous idea in our society[86] even today. Chastity is still a virtue as well, but its propagation is suffering a different, less sustained fate than monogamy. Because society allowed for the introduction of forms of sexuality[87] into a relationship, exclusivity is introduced as a measure of protection for the sexual participants.

Dating as we know it is baiting people into a trap; it's downright harmful to its participants. There are basically only two ways out of a dating relationship and half of them are inherently painful. You are either going to change the status of your relationship by breaking up with the person you are dating, or you are going to change the status of your relationship by becoming engaged and married. Those are the only two ways out of dating once you have started that relationship. And let's not kid ourselves – most dating relationships end with a breakup.

If dating is so bad and my parents are ill-equipped to set me

---

85 At the college ministry where I used to work, we would give guidelines that stemmed from the Bible but included our own personal experiences and judgments as well. Most of the Christian dating books I've read, sermons/podcasts I've listened to, as well as Christian conferences I've gone to do this same thing as well to varying degrees. And they, for the most part, seem to have found a consensus.

86 Sort of... some might say that monogamy never has been desired by certain people all throughout history; I can't argue with this idea, but I will point out that desire and virtue are not synonymous.

87 If only kissing, making out, petting. People use the analogy of baseball bases sometimes; this harkens the idea of degrees of sexuality, some of which are acceptable, some of which are less so.

up in an arranged marriage, but I still want to get married, what in the world am I supposed to do?

The answer to this question is why I decided to write this book in the first place. Otherwise, I would just point everyone to Hiestand and Thomas's book *Sex, Dating, and Relationships: A Fresh Approach*.[88] Their book, in my opinion, is brilliant. If you read their book, you will see that I heavily borrow from their thought processes, yet the concepts aren't theirs – they're from the Bible. That's why I like them so much. But in case you don't make it to the footnotes, they were the last piece I needed in order to coalesce a useful, biblical, comprehensive[89] dating paradigm.

One more time, just for gusto, or in case you skipped[90] straight to this chapter, here is what I recommend: don't look to jump into an exclusive, committed dating relationship. The traditional dating model can lead to misplaced trust and unnecessary heartache. It openly invites sexual compromise. It forces you to choose one person and exclude everyone else in a less than optimal decision-making environment. It invites its participants into a false sense of security.

Don't get me wrong, the traditional relationship model can work to accomplish the goal of finding a spouse and entering into a healthy, God-honoring marriage relationship. I'm just convinced

---

88 *Sex, Dating, and Relationships: A Fresh Approach*, Hiestand, G., Thomas, J. Crossway 2012

89 Comprehensive in the way the car insurance industry uses the word. It doesn't cover everything, but it's going to cover a lot more; except you'll probably need to use all the stuff this covers, whereas if you get both flood damage and hail damage on your vehicle, you need to move (or stop moving, depending on your circumstances)

90 Go back and read the rest of the book. It will help you understand the reason behind everything in the next sentence. It will help you understand the necessity for everything in the following chapters. My mom wouldn't want you to skip anything I wrote. Your mom probably doesn't want you missing any of the content in this book.

that that is never the best way. I just think that every single time it has worked for people who have dated that way, no matter how well it was done, the whole process was harder and riskier for everyone involved than it had to be. You can date in the same manner as the rest of society (or a Christianized version of it, at least), but you are making the process unnecessarily hard on yourself. So, don't do that. Try this instead.

Step One: The Right Place at the Right Time

THE FIRST THING in pursuing a godly marriage relationship you will want to do is be around the right people. I would say step one represents one of the hardest mindset changes that you will face. This step will make sense as we talk more about it, but I suspect you will not realize how important it is. In fact, I would say this is the most important step of the entire process and you will find yourself miles ahead in every other step if you do this one right.

Step one: find and cultivate a healthy Christian community. This sounds simple, and you might think, "Check! I already have a church that I love! What's next? How do I find him?" But let's slow down and talk about this one a little more; we need to make sure that your Christian community is the type of healthy community that makes finding what you want in a marriage and spouse more likely and less arduous.

Why a Christian community? Because it's the most important thing you can surround yourself with: people who get to know and influence you, people who realize who they are in relation to God, realize their own brokenness, and are relying on God's strength for their reconciliation with Him and relationships with other people. People who do this are likely going to be at peace more of the time; they will be at peace with God, themselves, and other people. People like this will provide relational support for you in a unique and selfless way.

Christian community is important because the world is never going to stop shouting all sorts of messages at you and you will need other people to help mute the noise. You will need other people to remind you of what is true. You are going to be around people who share a common reality (some would say worldview) with you, but I don't think all worldviews are created equal. A worldview grounded in the teachings of Jesus Christ will be one that will prepare you much more thoroughly to find what you're looking for in a relationship without unnecessary resistance.

There are a lot of people out there who are nice, and a lot of other community organizations have kind, genuine, smart people who are selfless and may care about you, and frankly Christian communities are far from perfect. However, Christian communities are uniquely equipped for your benefit in ways that your sorority or running club or honors college or cross-fit group is not. In all those other groups, acceptable truth is governed by consensus. What you want to govern your life is truth determined by the Word of God. And by the way, if your Christian community is more of a consensus-based truth group than based on truth from the Word of God (and there are definitely Christian communities in both camps), then your Christian community is not a healthy one. And as always, you can still find what and who you're looking for in a less healthy theological environment, it will just be much more difficult than it needs to be.

Your healthy Christian community also needs to be varied. If your community is only made up of people who are around your age and in a similar station of life as you, that is not enough; you need a broader, more developed community than that. You are going to want to develop relationships, real relationships, with lots of different people. Your community certainly needs to have people who are in the same station of life as you, but it also needs to have people who are older and younger, people who have kids and don't have kids, people who are in college and are not college-age, people who have grown kids out of the house, and people whose kids are still living at home.

In other words, if you are in college and more than 80% of the time you spend on relationships is spent with other college students, your environment is not optimal for finding a mate.

You need to invest time in these varied groups of people. You need to spend time serving them in ways that you are able, encouraging them in their own relationships with God and other people. You need to get to know this wide variety of people at a much more substantial level than any information which might be able to be gathered from their social media accounts. Also, and this should go without saying, you need to allow yourself to be known by these people as well. Let them get to know you.

There are so many reasons why you should want to do this, and I'll get to more of them later, but I will only highlight one now. The more people you connect with on a truly emotional level, the much less likely you will be to find yourself emotionally dependent on any one person. If the person you're dating is the person who provides the majority of your emotional support, something going wrong within your relationship will endanger your very emotional stability, to say nothing of the inherent imbalance in relationship to begin with. It will be very hard for you to be able to find the type of relationship you actually want if the bulk of your emotional weight is on any one person. Some day you will be married, and even then, you are not going to want to have one hundred percent of your emotional support in your spouse. It is very difficult for a healthy relationship to exist for any length of time when it is outside of a healthy community.

You need to develop relationships across age and life seasons. Now keep in mind that the way you connect with the seven-year-old kid you babysit will have to be different than the way that you will be able to connect with his grandmother or your best friend, but you might be surprised how beneficial it is for both of you if each of you knows a few things about each other that make you happy. You might be surprised at how sincere interactions with children can benefit you as much as, or in some ways, more than interactions with people who are your age or older.

You need to connect with people who are older and younger than you. The benefits to both of you will be myriad. Most of the time older people in Christian community have incredible wisdom that they need to dispense; undispensed wisdom makes its holder go stale. In other words, wise people are better off when they get to share their wisdom with others. The recipient is better off because he or she is that much wiser. It goes both ways. If you are the wiser person than the teenager you're spending time with, you will benefit from being able to give guidance and contextualize the truths of God to someone who isn't as far along in life as you. Also, if you're spending time with someone who is younger, hopefully you will be more likely to spend time in God's Word so instead of sharing your well-meant opinion that is being at least subtly influenced by the world, you can point that person to biblical, soul-curing truth.

You also need to connect with people who have different education levels and affluence than you. Developing a Christ-centered relationship with people in these different categories will be beneficial to your perspective. You need to have some of the underlying things you believe in challenged. Give time to people who are on both sides of the affluence scale from which you exist. Besides the fact that this is what the members of a healthy Christian community do, personally, your mindset about people in general will improve. And once again, I'm not talking about going to a homeless shelter once a month to serve soup (although, I think that's a noble thing and I don't want to discourage anyone from doing that). What I'm talking about is developing a genuine, sustained connection over time with another person who is engaged in Christian community with you. Keep especially in mind, you only have 168 total hours in your week this week, so if you are going to increase the amount of time you spend with certain people, time with other people or things will have to decrease.

You need to connect with people who are of a different race or ethnicity. Sadly, this can be especially hard in some Christian communities, sometimes even harder than connecting with people who are of different levels of affluence. Sometimes, your church is only made up of people who are of the same ethnicity as you are. Sometimes, your church exists specifically for that reason. However hard making these connections within Christian community is, they are worth it, if only in the context of finding the type of relationship you actually want. If you learn to connect in a real way with people who are culturally and ethnically different than you are, in a way that is authentic and vulnerable, the type of listening and empathy you will necessarily have to develop in order to sustain these relationships over time will serve you well in any genuine relationship you find yourself in for the rest of your life. Plus, you will be much less likely to exhibit implicit bias or prejudice, and that's a win for everyone.

And of course, you do still need to spend time with people who are your same age and station in life. I'm not going to spend a lot of time on same age, same gender but I will say that there are people who only spend time with people of the opposite sex, or they seem to feel more comfortable with people of the opposite sex. If this is you, as you intentionally cultivate the variety of your community, you need to start spending more time with people of your same sex. I understand, they might all just be jocks and meat-heads who spend all their time talking about sports, and you don't even care about sports. Or girls who only seem to like coffee dates and shopping. But for the sake of a healthy Christian community and you being in a position to find the long-term romantic relationship you eventually want, having people in your life of the same sex who you can push towards Christ, and who can draw you towards Christ, is crucial. Also, as far as connecting with them, care more about them in relation to Christ than whether or not all the other girls your age are just boy-crazy, or shopaholics or obsessed with monster trucks; or if all the other guys your age care only about the latest video game, or are just girl-crazy, or are obsessed with the Food Network and Home and Garden Television; if you have a pursuit of Jesus in common, start there. If they are not as far along in their faith as you are, start there. But don't come up with an excuse to primarily connect with people of the opposite sex while you are developing community. This is a huge mistake. You need to have friends who are the same sex as you are.

You also need to spend time with people who *are* of the opposite sex. I will have to spend a little more time with this one because it needs more detail. Pay attention. Step one is about developing a healthy Christian community. Step two is find the person you are going to marry. IT IS A HUGE MISTAKE TO START STEP TWO BEFORE YOU HAVE ESTABLISHED STEP ONE. I understand how hormones work. I understand what all the television shows tell you incessantly. I get it that from the bottom of your heart, you want to be in an exclusive, committed relationship. I get that. I really do. I also presume to know the patterns you have seen and practiced your whole life up to now. For the sake of not making it unnecessarily more difficult and complicated than it has to be for you to get what you actually want in a future exclusive relationship, I implore you to pay attention and don't miss this part.

First of all, when you are developing Christian community, what you should not do is look at the process of interacting with members of the opposite sex as vetting or reserving potential future mates. Please do not choose to (or choose not to) develop real, authentic connections with people of the opposite sex with the idea that he or she could be your future mate. This one mental shift will do you a world of favors as you do look to eventually end up in a healthy marriage relationship. It will help you in the selection, as well as in your interactions.

One of the biggest problems I run into with guys is that they don't know how to talk to girls. There was this one time a college freshman came into my office. He liked this girl, but he couldn't bring himself to talk to her because he would always get so nervous any time he was in the room with her. This particular girl was also a college freshman who I'd known since she was in the fifth grade: the kindest, sweetest girl around, and actually a great choice for any guy. She was confident about who she was, but not intimidating by any measure. I was thinking, "I can't imagine someone being too intimidated to talk to this sweet girl," because I had known her for as long as I had and because I'm years older than her, but the fact of the matter is I too have been in the same position as this freshman guy. When you are interested in a girl, it can change everything. You forget how to act, how to speak, how to just be *normal*. You can't act normally with her or speak naturally to her or behave normally around her because you think of her differently than everyone else.

Some of the very shy guys have probably found themselves in situations where they felt totally normal around a girl until one day they realized that they "like" her for whatever reason. And, in an instant, it becomes impossible to talk to her or even make eye contact. If this is you, this is a problem because you will have a very hard time getting to know someone with whom you are unable to make eye contact or with whom you have difficulty communicating. Also, as an aside, even though I'm going to spend the remainder of this book trying to convince you to think and operate in a way that this doesn't matter: ladies, sometimes none of the guys interact with you, not because they are not interested in you, but because they *are* interested. He likes you so much, he can't even approach you. This paradox exists exactly because of the current dating paradigm and the accidental results it creates. The way society dates makes it harder to find a spouse, and it makes it harder for the person who might be your spouse to find you. We need to stop making it harder.

Pay close attention to this next part because I'm going to tell you how you need to interact with people of the opposite sex in a way that will lead you more directly to the outcome you actually want. I will also tell you how not to interact with people of the opposite sex as to lead you more directly to the outcome you want. What I tell you here is going to challenge most, if not all, of what you have ever seen and what I am about to describe will probably also run contrary to your natural instincts. If you want what's best for you in the long run without accidentally making it harder to get there, please pay close attention and then think about what you read.

What Dating Should Look Like

Let's go over the general principles first, and then we can talk about some specific examples to highlight the principles. Keep in mind that right now you are developing community. You are not trying to find someone to be your boyfriend or girlfriend. You are not trying to find a person who might be your spouse someday. You are developing friendships in a Christian community.

Society tells us that men and women can't be friends. This is simply not true. What I'm going to try to outline here is how men and women can be actual, literal, legitimate, true friends, with no reservations or hesitations. Not only can men and women be friends, but both the men and women are better off when they have friends of the opposite sex – and inversely, both men and women are probably worse off when they don't have friends of the opposite sex.

If this process is going to work the way you want it to, if this is going to work at all, you must not single out only one, or even two members of the opposite sex with whom to pursue friendship. Men, I need you to listen well for a minute. You need to seek to be friends with even the girls to whom you are not physically attracted. And yes, it's okay to recognize that they are pretty. It's not okay to mentally linger on their beauty. It's not okay to lust. It's not okay to treat them differently because of the way they look. It's not okay to ignore certain girls because they don't look a certain way or have a certain body type. Not okay at all. If you are that shallow right now, just stop.

Guys, when you start spending time with girls one-on-one, make it your goal to try and not go out with the same girl twice in a row. One of the side goals of this method is to directly attack a problem that I see all the time. There are some absolutely phenomenal Christian women who are being rock stars in the Lord, but they are not being asked out on dates. There are some phenomenally clueless Christian men who don't even know what amazing can be in a woman because they eliminate even the chance of getting to know certain women for any number of reasons (and I'm trying to be kind here – there is usually only one reason and it has everything to do with looks). Everyone is worse off because of it, men. Everyone.

When you decide to begin participating in activities with

members of the opposite sex, you will want to diversify the people you spend time with. There are several benefits to diversifying that you will personally experience, even beyond the fact that you will be strengthening the entire church by caring well for other people.

This whole process of redefining what dating is and how to go about it will be easier if other people are participating with you. But this whole process will still be worth it even if you are in it by yourself. I would say, however, share this book with all your friends. Share it with your older mentors. Share it with people who are younger than you. Share it with your pastor. You might be the first person to break the patterns of culture, but other people who share the same values as you will probably want to join in once they understand what you are trying to do, and the more people you have running against the patterns of culture, the easier it will be. This is the same with every aspect of Christian living.

Broaden your pool and you will learn to be less nervous.

For those of us who do find it hard to approach and talk to that certain someone now, if you train yourself not to see anyone as unapproachable, when the time comes, no one will be unapproachable. You don't have to be concerned with messing up your future chances because you are not worried about a potential romantic future. You don't have to try to prove yourself worthy of another date because you won't be looking for another date. In the same way you probably feel much less pressure when you are getting to know a same-sex friend because the societal pressures and sexual tensions are not at play, you can choose to have the very same mindset as you develop opposite-sex friendships with the same goals and intentions as you would with a platonic same-sex friendship.

Broaden your pool and you will be able to practice chivalry.

This next benefit goes more for the male than the female, but that's only because this area is one where the male is generally more lacking. You can get some really good practice in behaving properly when you spend time with friends of the opposite sex. You can learn how to listen to another person well. Different people communicate in different ways and if you are spending time with lots of different people, you will be forced to learn how to listen well and how to communicate with patience. This is something that you will be developing in every relationship within your community, whether it is with the young married couple you get dinner with once a month or the empty nesters who act as some of your primary mentors; but this lesson will be particularly acute as you interact one on one with members of the opposite sex in the same station of life.

Broaden your pool and you will accidentally be exposed to awesomeness.

This is one of the biggest benefits of spending time with lots of different people. You will give yourself a chance to get over yourself and will probably accidentally become friends with some truly spectacular people who you would not otherwise get a chance to get to know. Maybe you wouldn't take the time to decide to spend time with him or her because of something superficial, or maybe you would intentionally avoid him or her because of something superficial (or perhaps something not superficial). If you are one to date one person at a time, you get to know only that one person really well, but you are less likely to discover admirable qualities in other people within your community – another person may have the same sense of humor as you, or think deeply about things the same way you do, or may have an incredibly refreshing eternal perspective. Would you ever want to date him or her? It doesn't even matter. You might see the joy of the Lord in someone in a real way which you may have only glimpsed, or perhaps completely missed out on otherwise. Seriously, there are a lot more people who are downright impressive than you realize. Not to mention, other people might be missing some things that are incredible about you, for the same reasons you miss those attributes about other people.

This is also a great time for you to discover characteristics you enjoy in members of the opposite sex without the pressure to have to like more things than you don't like. You will have the freedom to simply appreciate the person without any pressure to identify deal-breakers.

Broaden your pool and you will learn how to be less awkward.

The more different people you spend time with, the more likely you will learn to be less awkward. Some people don't have the problem of being awkward, but for the rest of us, broadening your interactions with members of the opposite sex will give you a chance to be charitable, joyful, peaceful, patient, kind, good, faithful, gentle and self-controlled in lots of different contexts. If you are all those things at the same time, it is impossible to feel awkward. It's true. Try it out for yourself. Do those nine things at once and the people around you will feel comfortable. If you are making the people around you feel comfortable, awkwardness cannot exist. By the way, this little nugget might be worth the price of this book, or worth the time it took you to borrow it from the library.

Broaden your pool and you will have some great stories to tell someday.

If only because the rest of society isn't going to do it this way, you're going to have a story to tell someday. Because you are going to be exposed to lots of different personalities, lots of different temperaments, lots of different family histories and lots of different depths of faith, you will be creating memories that will stay with you for a long time. Also, you may be developing a shared history with someone who could quite possibly be in your life in a real way for a very long time, especially if you don't end up marrying him or her someday.

Broaden your pool and you will have some great friends that you probably would not have otherwise.

I can't belabor this point too much. When you take the time to truly develop a Christian community, one day you will look up and have an incredible, supportive, varied, God-honoring community of friendships. If you are the person who makes other people feel included by deliberately looking to develop those friendships with people who "aren't your type," you will be cultivating a culture of people who are inclusive and accepting. You are treating the person you spend time with like he or she is a blood brother or sister. If you are out dancing, you dance as if he were your literal brother. If you don't already dance with your siblings, consider starting (they are probably the best ones to practice dancing with anyway).

The topics you pick to talk about need to be the types of things you would feel comfortable bringing up if your pastor were there as well. Also, keep in mind, you will be best not asking, "When was your first kiss?" or any similar question that will obviously tempt or trigger his or her mind to think romantically. This also means, you are probably not going to want to take a long moonlit walk on the beach with someone of the opposite sex, even if you do that sort of thing with your siblings all the time. I'm not going to be able to exhaust every overt situation you will want to avoid because they are different for everyone, but I will only caution you that you have to be wise. I imagine that most people who are looking to sabotage themselves will see the path of sabotage before they decide to walk down it. You'll see the path, and then you'll start justifying to yourself why it's not so bad (after all, the sunscreen needs to get on her back somehow).

There is no right way to go about trying to establish this type of genuine friendship with someone of the opposite sex. However, there are definitely ways to go about it that are unadvised. I'm about to lay out some general principles and questions I would anticipate based on where these friendships need to deviate from the way conventional dating operates, and where it is okay to stay the same. For the most part, the rules you should follow in your interactions with members of the opposite sex should be the same as if you were spending time with someone of the same sex, for the most part. Everything you do should be completely above reproach. This means you must always act in a way that puts you beyond the reach of blame, discredit or disgrace. The most convenient example of this is if you are hanging out at someone's house of the same sex alone at night, and judgement is left up to the imagination of someone who doesn't know your upstanding morals or know what is going on inside; no one would be able to justifiably call your character into question. However, if you are hanging out at someone's house of the *opposite* sex alone at night, you might not be doing anything that will cause regret or shame later, but a reasonable person could reasonably think otherwise. At every point, you need to operate beyond the farthest stretches of blame.

Okay, so you get it. Avoid situations that might bait or tempt you into any type of moral failure. But what about other, more innocuous situations. Who pays for dinner? To answer questions like this, I would say two things. 1) Do what you would do if she were another she or if he were another he. If you're anything like most people, this depends on a lot of things. If you came up with the idea for the activity and it costs more than you think the other typically would spend on such an activity, you might consider treating the other person. If you have a full-time job and you're doing something with someone who is still in school or is in a less fluid financial situation, consider treating the other person. If you are a generous person, consider treating the other person. If you are not a generous person but you want to be, consider treating the other person. If you can't pay for the whole thing, pay in proportion to what you are able.

But also, let the other person treat you. If you are a female and you expect the male to pay, that will be fine for what we go over in the next chapter – in other words, that will be a perfectly fine expectation if he is pursuing you romantically; but that pursuit is not happening right now. And just so there is zero confusion, if he is following this advice, you will not be confused as to his intentions. In the meantime, you get to give him the benefit of the doubt as to what his intentions really are. Allowing him to pay for your meal or activity is not you accruing a debt that you will have to repay *in any way* in the future. Any type of reciprocal repayment for kindness is not what Christian community is about. We don't give to people because people gave to us first. We don't give to people because we might want or need to receive something on some future date. We give to people because we have the example from Jesus Christ giving his life for us when we didn't want to repay Him and couldn't repay Him even if we wanted to. The kindness of a Christian is a reflection of Jesus Christ. Therefore, we can receive kindness without reservation. So basically, don't be afraid to pay for the other person and don't be afraid to have the other person pay for you. The two keys are to give graciously and receive graciously; and communicate beforehand, especially if you are expecting the other person to pay for any portion of the activity. A little hint: if you didn't plan the activity and your sensibilities don't allow for you to ask the other person directly about payment, you can ask something like, "How much money should I budget for this activity?" And if you are financially able, bring double that amount and pay for the other person as well!

Is there still an expectation for the male to initiate and plan the interactions?

In a word, no. Men, you should be looking for opportunities to practice taking initiative as well as looking for opportunities to grow in your planning abilities. But this is also situational. If you initiate the activity, consider yourself responsible for all the planning involved in the activity. But just like you might find yourself doing with a friend of the same sex, you might be inclined to share in the planning. Just be sure to communicate clearly what your expectations are. Also, be sure to communicate clearly if you are expecting the other person to communicate clearly and he or she has yet to do so.

What then should we do?

Great question. It's probably going to be coffee or something with a very low planning/cost/expectation factor. If it's anything else, invite more people. Your default should be to invite more people, even if it's only one other person. There are so many advantages to doing things in groups. If at all possible, go with more people. If you are an introvert, interaction is hard, and lots of people are overwhelming – go in groups of three. Try not to use up a great group activity on just one other person if you could have shared the experience with others.

You want to do low planning/cost/expectation because you're not looking to do anything more special for this person than you would for anyone else at this point. You are looking for activities that have the potential for repeatability with other, different people. You are also looking for circumstances that you both will enjoy. Ideally, you are going to want to pick an activity that allows for or encourages talking and interpersonal interaction. Movies and plays are easy, but they are not ideal because you can't have a conversation in the middle of the movie. You will want to give the majority of your attention to the other person, not to a performance. Of course if *West Side Story* is being performed in your town by a professional traveling group and the two of you are the only two who like *West Side Story*, go to *West Side Story*; but also, drag some other people along with you because it's *West Side Story* and anyone who doesn't like *West Side Story* probably just hasn't seen a good performance of it before.

What if I want to develop a relationship with someone of the opposite sex who is not a Christian?

I think this is a great idea to develop relationships with non-Christians! If you know for sure that they do not profess Christ as their only hope and means of salvation, invite them all the time to group activities. You can get to know them and share experiences with a non-Christian with other Christians around as well. There may be a level of depth and transparency that this friend of yours might not feel comfortable sharing with other people around with whom he or she does not already have a strong connection. I understand this, however prudence dictates that the potential benefit of spending one-on-one time with a non-Christian of the opposite sex will almost never come close to the potential detriment of that one-on-one time with a non-Christian. The only difference between a Christian and a non-Christian is that a non-Christian does not have the Spirit of God in him or her to direct good intentions and squelch not so good intentions. It's only one difference, but it has gigantic implications. By the way, you have the freedom to be much more vulnerable in connecting with non-Christians of the same sex as you; so, don't hesitate to involve your opposite-sex Christian community in your opposite-sex non-Christian friendships. One last caution. If the non-Christian (or a Christian for that matter) continually tries to isolate you from a healthy Christian community, this is a big warning sign and you should proceed only with extreme caution.

The three T's

Now I'm going to give you the keys to intimacy. There are three primary factors that you can adjust in your interactions with another that have a direct bearing on your level of romantic intimacy with the other person. I tell you about these here because you need to be aware of how you're using them so that you don't misuse them. If you are unaware, you might accidentally act in a manner that will lead you towards a relationship that demands commitment before you are ready. These things are pretty intuitive, so you could figure them out for yourself, but taking the time to articulate and define them will only sharpen the knife of their effectiveness.

Also, if you are trying to win someone's heart (which we are going to discuss in later chapters) these are going to be the things you will be augmenting. And one last warning before we get into it: any time you adjust the way you use these keys, whether you are intentionally aware of what you are doing or not, you are manipulating the other person; make no mistake about it – it is manipulation in the same way that smiling at someone manipulates them into returning the smile, or saying hello to someone will almost always get the other person to say hello back to you. However, if you are aware of how to manipulate someone and you intentionally do it for your own benefit or gain, or without regard for the other person, you might be entering into the realm of harming both God and the person you are manipulating. Or in the words of my Uncle Ben, "With great power comes great responsibility."[91] Please don't abuse your power.

Time

Pay attention to the amount of time you spend with the other person. It does not matter if it's quality time or one-on-one time. It does not matter what you are doing with the other person. The more time you spend with someone, the more comfortable you will be around that person. The more time spent, the more familiar you will be. Spend enough time with someone and it will lead to increased intimacy, as long as you are not thinking unfavorably about them the entire time. One-on-one time will make intimacy develop more rapidly, but any time you spend time with someone in any context, the time aggregates. Be careful.

Also, be aware of the context in which you spend time with the other person. Spending time alone in private will lead to increased intimacy in relationship much more quickly. Spending time late at night, whether you are with other people or not, will much more quickly lead to increased intimacy in the relationship. Spending time while either of you is experiencing increased stress or duress or crisis or is otherwise inordinately emotionally vulnerable will lead to increased intimacy in the relationship. Finally, spending time together in unfamiliar environments or when both of you are

---

91 He's not really my uncle. It's a *Spiderman* reference.

discovering an entirely unique experience will lead more quickly to increased intimacy in the relationship.

Touch

Pay attention to the way and the amount you touch the other person. At this point, it should be clear to you that sexual relations means any touching with sexual intent or undertones, and that for the sake of getting what you really want in a way that is not more difficult than it needs to be, sexual relations are completely off limits before and outside of a true committed relationship. Even outside of intent, be careful. Is holding hands something you can do with a sibling and it doesn't mean anything? Are you a hugger regardless of who it is? Do you simply have the propensity for touch? Is it how you best receive love? Everyone needs to be touched, and some more than others (and some less than others...). All the touching might be innocent, and I hope it is, but it may not be innocent for the other person. Regardless, touch over time leads to intimacy.

Talk

Finally, pay attention to your talk. You need to talk to the other person, without question, but the content of what you talk about is very important to be aware of. We've already talked about flirting and how that is actually harmful, so you understand the danger of amorous behavior. Amorous speech is a specific subset of amorous behavior. Most flirting is done with words. You will want to avoid talking about anything that might lead either your or their minds to romantic topics. Some of the more common topics that you will want to avoid are: first celebrity crush, first kiss, most romantic vacation, what you're looking for in a mate, basically any topic of conversation ever broadcast in the date situations in TV shows like *The Bachelor* and *The Bachelorette*, any talk about weddings or future kids, and even though we are in the middle of reclaiming and redefining what dating is, best/worst dates.

We are warned a couple of times in the Bible to be very careful about the things we say; what comes out of our mouths in the words we speak is terribly powerful. Please don't use your words to draw someone into a mental place that will be more likely to allow for moral compromise. Be aware and don't allow anyone else to do that to you. If they do, give the benefit of the doubt that the person you're talking with is not intentionally trying to manipulate you. Society saturates us with this type of talk, so you might not even be aware you are doing it, or you might have thought that there was nothing wrong with it until now. Either way, you need to be aware.

Some of the T's are unavoidable. Some of them you shouldn't entirely avoid. When combinations of the three T's are experienced with the others, their effect is amplified. As you are developing relationships with people of the opposite sex, particularly if they fall in your particular "potential spouse" demographic, you will need to pay close attention to the volume and manner in which you are using time, touch and talk to interact. Whether you are aware of it or not, these three things will communicate loudly your implied intentions with the other person. Now that you are aware, please do not neglect paying attention to these measures, and please do not abuse them.

When can we do it again?

When you start spending time with people of the opposite sex, you need to be sure to communicate that you are not looking to make one-on-one interactions a regular thing. You want to avoid the perception of exclusivity, even if you don't intend to create exclusivity by the frequency or repetitiveness of time you spend with the other. If he or she is your "best friend," as best friends, the two of you will want to continue to spend time in groups of three or four or more. If the two of you aren't dating but want to spend all your time together, what you can do is encourage one another to develop authentic, meaningful relationships with members from the broader church community. The same principle about spending time with the broader church community applies even if your best friend is the same sex as you. However, if your friend is the same sex as you, it's much less pertinent to intentionally not spend consecutive one-on-ones together.

Ladies, if a guy seems to start singling you out to spend one-on-one time, you will be better served to tell him no when he asks you again, and to tell him why. Explain to him the importance of avoiding deciding on one person that would only lead to the false commitment of the dating relationship. Tell him, "I am not looking to get into a dating relationship and since my emotions are susceptible to attachment whether I intend to be attached or not, I need to say no to your date. I don't want to put myself in the position of wanting to be exclusive with you when it's not the right time for that. Why don't you set up a group activity and include several people and I would love to be a part of that."

What about texting?

A special word on texting. Electronic communication such as texting or instant messaging still counts toward time spent together even though you (usually) are not in the same room as the texting is taking place. The time of day or night also matters when you are texting someone of the opposite sex. The later into the night you spend texting someone of the opposite sex, the more that relationship is one that will lead to intimacy. You will start pulling on the heart strings of the other person if you find yourself regularly texting into the late hours of the evening, especially if your texts have no express purpose (texts that late almost never have a legitimate purpose). So basically, the only thing you really need to know is that it is not ever, ever, ever a good idea to find yourself playing truth or dare via Snapchat at 2 o'clock in the morning. Absolutely nothing good at all will come of it. There is nothing you need to say that can't wait until morning, or more likely probably can go without being said at all. Flirting via text or social media is still flirting, and flirting will not help you get to where you ultimately want to be.

Ladies, if he has reached the point where he has decided on you, he needs to be able to clearly articulate that to you before he begins his pursuit. If he has reached the point where he has decided on you and he hesitates to make his intentions known, has he really decided on you? If he has reached the point where he has decided on you, but he is too afraid or nervous to tell you, then he is not ready for a serious pursuit. This might sound harsh, but if you're talking about someone eventually winning your heart forever, you are going to want someone who knows how to clearly communicate to you his intentions.

Guys, if you have decided that one girl in particular is the one you would like to pursue and that the time to pursue is now, but you don't know how, hold on for a bit and I will explain exactly what you need to do in the next chapter. But keep reading because this step is more important than that one. And by the way, on the off chance that you think you're already at the point where you've decided, but you haven't developed community in the way I've described, I suggest you pump the brakes on that relationship and take the time to develop community in the way I suggest here. Whether you end up with the one on whom you have set your sights right now or not, you will be better off because of it. And either way, the path you take to finding what you really want in a romantic relationship will be an easier one to walk.

Group Activities/Dates

Group activities are better than one-on-one dates in almost every situation and circumstance. If at all possible, you need to try and replace most one-on-one dates with group activities. If you are looking to discern a person's true character, having other people around will really come in handy. If she is sweet to you because she is interested in you, but is cold and acerbic to everyone else who she doesn't want anything from, what do you think her personality is really like? Is he kind and thoughtful around you when you are alone, but a gaudy show-off when he's around you and all his friends? I can't tell you which one he actually is, but I know you don't want to be around someone whose character changes depending on who he's around.

Please don't misunderstand me, but also don't miss this. It's okay that you don't treat everyone exactly the same. You are going to speak in a high pitch to your infant nephew in a way that you absolutely would not to your college philosophy professor, but if you are gentle you are going to be gentle to both. If you are kind, your kindness will reveal itself in different ways to different people, but it will always reveal itself. If you are trying to establish a non-platonic romantic relationship with someone, you will be more likely to mask your negative characteristics with that particular person. If you are always in group situations, and you want anyone in the group to think you are patient, but you really are not, you will have to fool the whole group into thinking you are patient by being patient with everyone in the group. And there's the trick. If you are consistently patient with everyone over time, guess what? You are patient. You can fool any one person for a period of time, but you can't fool everyone all the time. More importantly, *you can be fooled* by anyone for a period, but it takes a particularly rare and scary person to fool everyone for an extended period of time. In other words, interacting in groups will protect you from being tricked into falling in love with a sociopath. Seriously. And even a little further, it's even more difficult to fool an entire church community for an extended period of time – keep that in mind.

Groups are also better because you don't have to be "on" all the time. When you are interacting with just one other person, you might feel pressure to be on most of the time. If the goal is getting to know other people, you don't always have to be the one to come up with the right questions to ask the other. Chances are, someone else will bring up an important or telling topic that will be very useful to you, and at the same time, you would have never thought to bring up on your own. It's easier to get to know people better when you're all in a group.

One more thing about groups, and this is really, really important. You absolutely need to be as inclusive as possible. You need to invite as many people to participate as possible. If there are annoying people in your potential friend group, or people who are of a different socio-economic class than the majority of the people in your usual group, or people of a different race, or people with different interests than most of the people you know, or anything at all, they need to feel included. A healthy church community is what you're going for here. Please, oh please, don't intentionally exclude people from your community. Maybe you will want to just create a group message and make it a rule that anyone who wants to can join. Then guard against yourself and other people in the group creating different subgroups that don't include everyone. These subgroups are impossibly toxic and harmful. This is easy to see when you're the one who is excluded, but for some reason it is much harder to see when you are one of the people in the in-crowd. Fight against this from happening. Once a group gets large enough and diverse enough, this almost always happens. Over time, these parallel selective groups are always harmful. Always. Healthy community is what you need to most easily find the person you will want to marry. Healthy communities are inclusive, not exclusive. Please, don't miss this.

No romantic action. No romantic intent. Not yet.

What you don't need to do: don't start going to a church to find the one you think you're going to be with. Don't start going to your church's singles group to find someone. The other people in the singles group probably won't appreciate it if you do. Also, if you don't attend your church's singles group because you think that's what everyone else is there to do, take a minute and get over yourself and start going to the group. You will be better off if you develop friendships with the people in the group. You'll be better off now and you'll be better off later. So will they. And so will the whole church.

When you do have an entire community of people around you, looking out for you, praying for you, your celebrations will be sweeter, and your disappointments will feel less disappointing. When you have an entire community of people around you, you will have emotional and social support that can help sustain or even help rehabilitate your own emotional and social health. When you have an entire community of people around you, you will be the beneficiary of years and decades of wisdom that you could not have possibly accumulated at this point in your life and that you might never accumulate. When you have an entire community of people around you, people who have gotten to know and love you, people who are praying for you, people who have your best interests in mind, then you will be in the best social circumstances to move on to step two: finding the person you are going to marry.

Step Two: The Right Person

NOW THAT YOU have established yourself in a healthy Christian community of people, you are in the best circumstances to move on to the step that you probably think you care about most. You might care about this step most, but it's not the most important of the steps. Don't skip building into a Christ-centered community. Don't miss the benefits and joys of having people support you as you move towards marriage. But before we get to marriage, we need to find the person you're going to marry.

We are going to talk about who to look for and how to find your mate. I think you will discover that in following this step, finding the one for you will be remarkably easier and demonstrably more effective than the way that everyone goes about it now. As always, as I describe the process, you might think that this is pretty intuitive, and you would be right. The hard part is finding the right circumstances, not finding the right person.

I'm going to go over a list of characteristics you will want to look for in everyone you meet. These are the things you need in the person you want to spend your life with. I can't stress enough that these are also the characteristics you will want to display in your own life and not simply for the sake of finding a spouse, though I guarantee that your spouse will be extremely grateful if you do have these qualities. More importantly, these characteristics are those that come only from God's Spirit in you, by God's grace given to you.

We need to work out these characteristics in our own lives, with fear and trembling, but we must remember that it is God who works in you, both to will and to work for His good pleasure.[92] When you identify these things in yourself, it is not by your own effort. As you identify these things in someone else, remember that these things are a gift from God in the life of a Christ-follower, and not by their own efforts. Before you look for specific character traits in another person, you need to identify and develop specific character traits in yourself. Every single aspect of your life will be better the more these characteristics reflect who you are as a person. I'll go over them one at a time.

Patience

This is the idea of treating the time someone else is asking or demanding of you as a precious gift to give, and not as a scarce treasure to protect. Patience comes into play when someone acts or thinks differently than you. Learn how to be okay with someone else being different. Does it bother you to show up places late, especially when it's not your fault? Patience is what it will take to refrain from being angry or upset with the person who causes you to be late. Do you get annoyed if someone you're with is always in a rush, maybe even to the point of rudeness? That annoyed feeling you feel, regardless of how justified you are in having it, is evidence of impatience. Now sometimes you will need to speak up about habits or behaviors that are negative or undesirable in the other person. You can recognize those things without being bothered by them. If you feel agitated or annoyed because of another

---

92 Philippians 2:12-13

in any context, you are experiencing impatience. The more patient you are, the better. Patience is taking the time to listen and understand someone else and is a clear indicator of a grace-filled person.

Kindness

When your patience does run short, as almost everyone's does at some point, kindness is when you choose to refrain from responding harshly to the person responsible for depleting your patience. Kindness is treating another person in a helpful manner. Kindness is being gentle towards the other person no matter how that other person is treating you, no matter the context. Kindness is deciding not to be mean, even when you might have justification, and choosing to have an optimistic and winsome attitude and outlook. Kindness is actively looking for and taking the opportunity to serve the other person in a meaningful way.

Don't Envy

For our purposes, envy comes across in a couple different ways. Envy is wanting what someone else has. Envy is seeing the other person's status, or possessions, or good looks or attention, and wanting that too. It might be that he or she has something that you want, but it doesn't have to be things. Is she the life of the party? Do you want to be the life of the party instead? Does everyone think of him as the smartest person in your year? Do you want everyone to think you are the smartest person in your year (because you actually are)? That is envy. Learn how not to do this. All your relationships will be better off if you aren't envious.

Envy is also feeling you have to prove that you are better than another person. When they tell the story about how they made all-district, you feel compelled to let them know you made all-state. If they share their love of painting, you make sure they know you won a regional art competition. When the person you're with tells you something good or impressive about themselves, learn how to fight the urge to automatically share something equally good or better about yourself. This is an impulse so many of us have. Learn to take pleasure from the successes and accomplishments of others without needing to one-up them.

Don't Be Boastful

You were fearfully and wonderfully made. You were. God did that. Now don't flaunt it. It's okay to share about things you've done or accomplished in life. Were you the valedictorian or salutatorian in your high school class? Congratulations! It was probably really hard work and you should be proud! But don't need for other people to be impressed by you. Don't use who you are or what you've done to gain the favor or approval of others. Many times, the tendency to use your accomplishments to impress other people is evidence of a misunderstanding of the source of your worth. Misunderstanding the source of your worth is a self-esteem problem. Remember, God did that.

Don't Dishonor Others

It goes without saying that you need to not be mean. Don't dishonor others. Don't intentionally embarrass someone else. Don't do anything that will intentionally bring shame to another person. What if your own parents got this one right all the time? Can you imagine, even if they're separated now, how much better their relationship might have been growing up? They might still be together if they had just gotten this one right. If they are still together, they might still be friends if they had just gotten this one right. Are they still friends even today? If so, I bet they got this one right. You need to practice honoring others, even when you don't feel like honoring them; honor them even when you have determined they don't deserve it. The thing is, dishonor is sneaky, and it comes in several different forms.

The contemporary millennial Christian culture has a very bad habit of dishonoring others, but it's disguised. Do you communicate with sarcasm? Many people do. It is easier and safer for you to say something mean, cutting or biting to someone only because you feel fond or endeared to that person. I have these two male friends who have a lot in common and are very good friends. Both guys love to hunt and fish and relax at the camp with a nice cold beer. They work together (that's how I know them) and they hangout often when they are not at work. Yet, I have never heard either of them say anything nice directly to the other. I can't count the number of times I've heard them say out loud to one another, "I hate you." I bristle every time I hear it even though I am 100% sure neither of them means it – and neither of them is the least bit confused as to how they actually feel about each other.

Do you ever tease someone else because you are 100% sure the other person knows you are being insincere in your meanness? Are the only people you make fun of the people to whom you are the closest? Do you think of your sarcasm as a type of special language that you and your close friends can understand between one another? You might even say that someone else speaks to you like this and you are not bothered in the least. And you might not be, but if you learn how to honor even your close friends with kind, positive words, you will be learning how to honor someone else in a way that is so powerful, it makes the world nervous.

Don't Be Self-Seeking

Learn how to put the needs of others before looking out for your own needs. Try not to do everything you do for your own benefit. I have the tendency to make sure I get what I think I deserve. I have the tendency to think about myself first; I certainly think of myself more than I think of anyone else. It's human nature, but more than that, it's a function of utility. If the saying, "Out of sight, out of mind" is true, and it inevitably is true given enough time, you will always be inclined to have yourself in mind because any time you are conscious, you are literally always in your own presence. No one else is around you as much as you are around you.

Even though we have the impulse to, we are not beholden to put ourselves and our wants and needs first. Doing things for your own gain to the detriment of others is a choice you get to make or not make. I am not suggesting that you completely disregard your own wants and needs because that is not healthy or wise, but learn to put the interests of others ahead of your own. Practice doing that.

Don't Be Irritable

People are imperfect and messy and will get on your nerves or try your patience. Being irritable is when you decide not to be kind when you run out of patience. Being irritable is when anger comes easily. Do you lose your temper quickly? Do you find you have extremely reasonable standards of which other people seem to regularly fall short? Does it sometimes seem like others are trying to intentionally get on your nerves? Here's a hint. They're not. You are just irritable (unless he is literally a middle school student... in that case, odds are he is actually trying to get on your nerves). "But," you say, "he literally acts like a middle schooler." No, he doesn't. You're just irritable. Stop. The good news is you can learn how not to be. The bad news is, it will probably require being around people who get on your nerves more frequently than you might otherwise. If you learn how to not be irritable, this will have a profound benefit on not only your future marriage, but in every relationship in any capacity on any level you ever have.

Don't Be Resentful

Did you know there is a difference between recognizing something is offensive and being offended? When someone else does something that can be clearly characterized as offensive, you have no control over his or her actions or intent, but you do have some measure of control over how you interpret and react to those actions. You don't have to feel ill will towards that thing you regard as wrong. We get to choose whether or not we will feel indignant displeasure. You get to choose. A big tool to not being resentful is learning how to give the benefit of the doubt to the other person.

You may think his actions speak for themselves. You say there is only one thing she could have meant when she said what she said. This is you being resentful, but you don't have to be. Resentment is something that occurs over time. The first time, you thought the best; the second time, you came up with a plausible excuse; but the third time! The third time, enough is enough. Or maybe for you it's more than three. For you, it's five times or seven times, or seventy-seven times. Learn how to not believe the worst in situations. Learn how not to harbor ill will. It will serve you well in the future and will help you greatly with the next characteristic as well.

Don't Keep Records of Wrongs or Hold Grudges

The closer you get to someone and the longer you are around that person, the more likely you will be to be hurt or offended by them. Don't keep track of when other people have wronged you. This one is virtually impossible if you're not a Christian. In order to not keep track, you have to feel like you aren't owed anything by the person who has wronged you. To not feel like the person owes you anything, you must forgive them completely. Non-Christians have the ability to forgive completely, certainly. But the capacity for a person to truly and fully forgive someone else is extremely limited without Jesus Christ. All the things we are talking about in this section are so difficult to be without Christ, but this one is in particular. Forgiveness is God's specialty. You need to learn how not to hold grudges. You need to learn how to forgive. Forgiveness creates the margin it takes for a relationship to flourish.

Don't Delight in Evil

There are a couple of ways people can delight in evil. You are going to want to avoid both. Do you take a little pleasure in seeing other people fail? Do you sometimes feel a little better about yourself when other people around you can't do something as well as you can? This finding enjoyment from the troubles of others is called *schadenfreude*. It is the opposite of compassion. It is delighting in evil. It is an impulse you will want to get rid of if you recognize it in yourself, an ugly tendency that so many of us exhibit from time to time. Evil does not need applause.

The second way to delight in evil is to derive pleasure from morally reprehensible behavior. If you are looking at pornography, you don't even need to be thinking about dating anyone in any capacity. Porn is the worst type of poison that will show up in your marriage in the worst ways possible; it will absolutely become a huge hurdle to finding the connection with your spouse you want to have. Porn changes the way you look at, think about, and interact with the opposite sex in the worst ways possible. Porn disrupts your relationship with God. There are other evils you might be faced with from which you are looking to or indulging in to get pleasure, satisfaction or fulfillment of your needs or wants – please don't find your delight in those evil things. But in this context especially, please avoid pornography. If you have never viewed it, please don't start. If you are using it, please stop before you get addicted. Get help. Be honest with someone about your need for help, specifically a mentor or church leader or someone in your life who can help guide you and keep you accountable. Please stop for the sake of your church community, yourself, your future spouse and the health of your relationship with God. Please stop.

Rejoice with Truth

Do you celebrate when you see God working in other people's lives? Do you celebrate when you see God has been working in your life? Matthew 6:33 reads, "But seek first the kingdom of God and his righteousness, and all these things will be added to you."[93] Rejoicing with truth looks like someone who is following the directive found in this verse. Rejoicing with truth is a demonstration in the value of anything that represents the righteousness of God. You need to become this person, a person who celebrates God's righteousness.

All of these character qualities are essential for you to become a person worth finding.[94] They are the building blocks on which a healthy, loving relationship founded in Jesus Christ exists. Not surprisingly, those are also very good character qualities to be on the lookout for in order to find a person worth finding. No one is going to be perfect at all of these at once. In fact, no one is going to be perfect at any of these at any given time. The question you need to ask yourself is, "Am I intentionally looking to exhibit these characteristics?" Most of these things will not come naturally

---

93 Matthew 6:33

94 For a more succinct listing, see 1 Corinthians 13

to you. What comes naturally is drifting further and further away from these if you are not aware. Finally, even if you do intentionally seek to exhibit these attributes, unless you are doing these things by the power of God, any good you gain in any one area of your life will come with negative side affects in another.

Step Three: Right for Each Other

THIS CHAPTER IS going to be a lot more gender specific in the instructions because starting now, the roles of men and women become distinctly different. Now is when you find the one you're going to marry.

You now have a healthy Christian community. You have an idea of crucial characteristics you need to have (first and foremost) as well as those characteristics which are desirable in a potential spouse. But, I know – you feel as if you are no closer to actually being married. In fact, since you are not in a dating relationship as you might have been at this point in the old way of doing things, you kind of feel like you are farther away from being married than you otherwise would be. So now what?

Now we get to talk about why you are not only closer to being married than someone who is not following this paradigm, but how you have set yourself up for an exciting transition from neighbors to marriage while avoiding most of the usual confusion and hurt and pain. This entire process minimizes this pain, confusion and frustration much more for the female than the male, only because in the current world of dating and relationships, the female generally disproportionately suffers all those negative things.

Men, the first thing you need to do is truly assess for yourself if you are ready to get married. If you are not ready to get married for whatever reason, do not start the process of choosing a spouse. If you choose someone and she chooses you back, but you don't get married after you've chosen each other, the only way to sustain that relationship is by entering into that fourth dangerous and artificial category of dating which is just as detrimental to the long-term health of both your current relationship and your future marriage relationship.

Get Wise Counsel

Now is one of the many places in your journey where your Christian community is crucial. Find three of the oldest[95], wisest men you know and three of the oldest, wisest women you know. Ask each of them to honestly tell you if they think you are ready to be married. If they are honest and they love you, they will tell you the truth. Pay very close attention if any of them tells you that he or she doesn't think you are. Find out why and figure out what you need to do to remedy their reasons. Proverbs 15:22 says, "Without counsel plans fail, but with many advisers they succeed." You want many advisers in your life when you are making decisions about marriage. Some of them need to be in your age and station in life, but some of them definitely need to be older and at least two life stages ahead of you. Even though this was written with the millennial in mind, no matter how old you are, get wise counsel.

If one of your trusted counselors does tell you that they think you're not ready, the reason you are given might be something like you need to finish school, although your status in school is only sometimes a reason not to get married. (In my personal opinion, still being in college in itself is not a good rule of thumb not to get married, but being in the maturity level of the typical college

---

95 Or most mature

student can very well be a good reason – I think our society in general is, on average, waiting later than it needs to before people get married, but I also think you're not allowed to rent a car until you're 25 for good reason).[96] If the reason you are given has to do with character issues and someone loves you enough to tell you, consider thanking them. Then search the Scriptures to find out what God's word says about whatever issue or issues have been identified by that loving person. It will be much easier for you to find a remedy for these things before you get carried away falling in love.

You need to pray about whether you are ready, and you need to be perfectly honest with yourself. If you think God is telling you that you are ready, but the wise, godly people in your life are telling you that you're not, you're probably mishearing God. People in their teens and twenties are notorious for accidentally mishearing God in situations where selfishness might be at play despite the holiest intentions. Listen to the older, wiser Christians in your life; especially if their names are Mom or Dad. And just a quick note for Mom or Dad: just because you are not ready for your child to be married does not mean that your child isn't ready. Sometimes "you're too young" is a good reason and sometimes it isn't. Also, keep in mind that you're having this conversation before he has begun any intentional pursuit. You don't have to guide him away from a bad choice. Instead, you get to guide him into a good one.

As you've been developing community, especially since you have been spending some of that time with people who are of marrying age, no doubt someone has jumped out at you. If not, that's okay too. If not, I would ask what things are you looking for? Are you paying more attention to character than looks? Are you paying

---

96 Most major car rental companies do allow people from the ages of 20-24 to rent vehicles, but the customer is generally subject to being charged a young renter fee.

better attention to the way she communicates with others than her social status? Did you notice the personality of someone that seems to fit yours as well? Or a sense of humor? Personality, sense of humor, or shared interests can be supplemental reasons to want to develop further interest in a woman, but only supplemental reasons. The primary things you need to look for are someone who is patient, kind, doesn't envy others, doesn't boast, isn't proud, does not dishonor others, is not self-seeking, is not irritable or resentful, someone who does not keep records of wrongs, and does not delight in evil but rejoices with truth; look for someone who always protects, always trusts, always hopes and always perseveres. A pretty face and a cute hair cut cannot be the basis for your choice, though those things are definitely a plus.

At this point, you should have somewhat gotten to know this girl with great character. You should have already spent lots of time in groups playing together, working together, serving together. You should already have developed a friendship in the context of community. You may have already done a one-on-one activity or two with her (and just as a reminder, you have also subsequently done one-on-one things with other girls in the context of a platonic neighbor as well). But mostly group activities and events. So, what's next?

But Who Specifically Do I Pick?

As you're getting to know people, you are learning about them because you care about them. But when it is time for you to start looking, and not before it's time, begin to be on the lookout for a specific type of chemistry in someone of the opposite sex. There are four other areas of compatibility that you need to be on the lookout for when you are trying to find the right person.[97]

---

97 Willow Creek Sermon: The 2010 Family Series: Dating

Spiritual Compatibility

When you become a Christian, Jesus Christ changes everything about you; your wants, dreams and desires change in a way that are not of this world. If you are a Christian male, do not look for someone who is not a Christian female to pursue for marriage. If you are a Christian female, do not accept the pursuit of a non-Christian male. If marriage is designed to reflect Christ and His Church, it would behoove the people in the relationship to see both Christ and His Church in the same light. Please do not tell yourself that so many things about the person are so great that you can figure this one out later. This is not an issue to overlook now and figure out later. Spiritual compatibility from the very start is of the utmost importance.[98]

If you are not a Christian, do not choose someone who is a Christian. If for some reason you do, the Christian is going to want you to change and become a Christian. You don't want to build a relationship with someone who necessarily wants you to be foundationally different. You are setting yourself up for disaster if you are attempting to build anything on two foundations that are not level. Whatever you build will be crooked and much more likely to fall should a storm come. Don't do it.

Be aware of nominal Christians. There are some people who claim Christianity because, culturally, it's just what you do. Some people are born into a family of Christians and learn all the rituals and talking points, but don't have a deep, profound desire for Jesus Christ. If you have a genuine faith in Jesus Christ, you need to make sure that the person you are considering has a genuine faith in Jesus Christ as well. How you spend your time, the things you think about, the way you spend your money, these are all things that nominal Christians will have an easy time understanding and

---

98 2 Corinthians 6:14

speaking about how Christ would call us to live in these areas, and he or she might even be able to point out Bible verses to prove understanding of the topics; you want to find someone who demonstrates the same types of changes in these areas you have seen in your life since you became a Christian, or at least someone who, for Christ's sake, is looking to make those changes and better align his or her life with Christ's life. When your faith is at the very core of your identity as a person, there are no areas of your life that aren't affected by it. This is why it is so important to seek spiritual compatibility.

Emotional Compatibility

As you are narrowing down the people you are considering, you will want to be sure to share your full stories with each other. It's not necessarily wise to share all the intricate details of the hardest parts of the story, but you shouldn't leave any parts out. You will want to talk even about the more painful areas. As you are talking and listening, you want to ask the questions, "Have you fully processed through what you have experienced?" "Are you ever overwhelmed by the emotions that come along with this story?" "Has what you've been through been redeemed?"

If you are at the point where you are talking about deep and potentially painful memories, hopefully this means you have a robust present relationship upon which you can reasonably trust that what you share won't be met with rejection or shame. That being said, if you hear something from the other person that seems to indicate they might not be ready for a committed relationship right now, you need to be careful not to unintentionally fuel any shame in the other person. Also, be very careful as to what type of thing triggers that assessment for you. Everybody has a past, and nobody's past is perfect. You would do well to be careful not to disqualify someone based on something that they did or that happened to them in the past. You should be concerned with how they dealt with those things from the past and how much of a present issue those things seem to be. When you're talking about making this type of relationship decision, you need to prayerfully consider (along with the counsel of older and wiser voices) when what you find out needs to be a valid reason to avoid a future romance. And no matter what, you need to be kind, communicative and respect that any red flags you might see from that person's past are the very things for which Jesus gave His greatest expression of love and sacrifice by dying on the cross. The other person not realizing the impact of Christ's sacrifice about any past indiscretions is the type of red flag you need to be on the lookout for, much more than any particular past circumstance or indiscretion.

Concerning present emotional temperament, there is no good way to say this: everybody is at least a little bit crazy. You need to figure out what brand of crazy he or she has and whether you can deal with it over time. If you think the person you are dealing with is not at least a little crazy, you are incorrect. You might call it a quirk or a little neurosis; you might even think that their crazy is cute. Whatever you do, you would be well served to identify what it is and determine if it's something you can live with. Seriously.

Compatibility in Communication

If your relationship is a car, communication is the tires. No matter how fast or new or powerful your car is, the tires are the only part of the car that come in contact with the road. Everything else might be more complex, but everything else rests on this. Bad communication can cause problems where there might not be otherwise. Good communication can identify and eliminate potential problems before those problems wreak havoc or mess anything up.

Here are some of the characteristics you are going to want to exhibit when you are talking with anyone, but especially in the context of a romantic relationship. Any time you are in conversation with someone else, give that person your full attention. Put down the phone. Turn off the television. Make eye contact. These are basics of social interaction that are so simple, people mess them up or forget to practice them all the time.

You want to listen first. You may have heard this before, but most people when they are in conversation are simply waiting for their turn to talk. Take the time to really listen to the other person. Take the time to be intentional about seeking to truly understand what the other person is trying to communicate to you. Ask good follow-up questions because you are genuinely interested in finding out more about whatever it is the person with whom you are speaking feels inclined to share. When you find yourselves talking about a contentious topic, give the other person a chance to get all their thoughts out before you get your thoughts in. The Bible tells us, "If one gives an answer before he hears, it is his folly and shame."[99] Your brain might move much faster than the person you're talking to talks and you might be sure you know what he or she is going to say before his sentence is finished No matter what, let him finish his own sentence. Don't cut him off. Don't finish the sentence for him. Regularly cutting someone off or jumping in at the end of sentences is one of the subtlest yet undeniable forms of disrespect. If you do this, it is to your folly and shame. Don't do this.

Don't speak too hastily. Don't just say whatever comes to mind for you because it's the first thing you think of saying. You can be both thoughtful and candid. If you find yourselves talking about a contentious topic, always be mindful not to say anything that will cause the other person to feel as if you are personally attacking him. Don't forget, words are like toothpaste. Once they are out,

---

99 Proverbs 18:13

no matter how hard you try you can never get them back in. As many of you know from experience, a harsh word has the particular characteristic of not being easily forgotten.

You want to be someone who does not get angry quickly or easily. If the person you're talking to doesn't understand how words are like toothpaste and it feels like he or she is speaking daggers, intentionally trying to injure you, it will serve you well if you are a person who can control your temper. Everyone does, and rightfully should, have their limits as to what they can endure before they become angry, but you want to be someone who takes a very long time before anger is sparked. We are given some great insights about this in the Bible. Proverbs 15:1 tells us, "A soft answer turns away wrath, but a harsh word stirs up anger."

There is a gigantic difference between not becoming angry and not expressing or displaying your anger. Good communication is not suppressing your anger. Bad communication is when you don't let the other person know that they have angered, wronged, or offended you. Bad communication is also when you talk to other people about what that person said or did before you first talk to the person who said or did it. It's thinking to yourself, "He should know what he did," and deciding not to tell him how what he did made you feel. You get zero credit for being able to pretend not to be angry or being an expert at hiding your anger. "Fake it 'til you make it" doesn't apply in this situation. Maybe this means you need to calm down and collect your thoughts before you say anything to the offending party, but you still need to be able to communicate your feelings and emotions. You want to be a person who can calmly communicate when you feel a certain way based on the offending actions of another.

You also want to be a person who can give honest, sincere compliments. You want to be a person who expresses gratitude when you are thankful. This skill of speaking kind words without a hint of sarcasm or irony, or spoken without a matching insult, seems to be harder and harder to find. Sometimes it seems like it makes people equally uncomfortable to both give and receive genuine compliments. You want to be a person who can give sincere compliments and feel comfortable doing so. You want to be a person who can also receive sincere compliments without half-rejecting, deflecting or being awkward about it.[100]

When you have a hard thing to say, you need to be able to say it clearly and truthfully. You also need to always communicate hard things with the meekness and grace the situation warrants. And in case you are wondering, there are no situations where graceless, truth-only statements are warranted. None. You must have both truth and grace when you are confronting someone. Truth without grace is mean. Grace without truth is meaningless. And you must have courage to speak up in the first place. Speaking the truth with grace in a timely manner is crucial for good communication.

Communication is Key

The above relationship qualities are what you should be seeking to practice in every situation you're in, regardless of with whom you are interacting. These are skills which can be developed, not switches to be flipped when you need them. By the time you are in a committed relationship, you will need them. You do not want to wait until you are in said committed relationship to start developing these skills, or to discover that you don't have them. You need to start practicing now.

One last word about compatibility. If you are bad at these things, the goal isn't to find someone else who is equally bad at them; that would only be a recipe for disaster. If someone is bad at communicating in any or a few of these ways, it doesn't mean that

---

100 By the way, here's how: just smile and say, "Thank you."

person is hopeless. These are skills that can be developed. What it does mean is that interacting with that person will be harder than it has to be, and it might come at a great cost to you. Good communication is so important. You are going to want to get this one right yourself, and you are going to want to find this in any person you are considering. Good communication prevents so many preventable things.

Physical Attraction

You need to be physically attracted to one another. Don't try to over-spiritualize yourself and say that looks don't matter. Looks do matter, but a word of caution: chances are you have been putting WAY too much emphasis and importance on looks. As you begin to search for a person who you would like to spend the rest of your life with, his or her looks should be no more than a footnote in what you're assessing. I once read a very clever book about using math to find love in which the author poignantly put it this way, "Plump lips and big biceps might be nice to look at now, but they won't be much help at 4 o'clock in the morning when your baby's diaper needs changing, or in sixty years' time when your catheter bag needs replacing."[101] Good looks are neither permanent nor are they particularly utilitarian.

The Bible reminds us that beauty is fleeting. The thing about looks is gravity works on everyone and it always wins. The way she looks now is not the way she will look 20 years from now. Her looks are not one of the planks on which you build your relationship because we know that is one trait that will definitely change. Also, when she has a shining godly character and you still have a strong relationship 20 years from now, you will find her attractive

---

101 Fry, Hannah, *The Mathematics of Love: Patterns, Proofs, and the Search for the Ultimate Equation* (TED Books)

because chemistry, affection and the purity of intimacy have a way of making the object of your affection physically attractive.

But for now, put physical attraction on the list; just make sure it's not too high up there. Don't value this too highly. Because while looks go away, true godly character almost never goes away.

Other Considerations

If you find someone who is of a different demographic than you, I need to give you some special cautions. I'll take them one at a time.

Age – there is nothing in the Bible that gives any prohibitions on there being a wide age gap between two people engaged in an exclusive romantic relationship. Society, on the other hand, has very distinct opinions on the matter. If you are looking to enter into a relationship with someone who is not your age, proceed with caution and proceed with counsel. The younger you are, the more likely it will be for problems to arise based on age difference. The greater the age difference, the more likely it will be for problems to arise as well. There is no guarantee that you will have problems based on age, but it's a difference that needs to be acknowledged.

More often than age, though, are problems that arise in direct relation to age; things like whether or not one of you is still in school while the other has already graduated may become a problem, or if one of you has already been married and divorced, or has children already, or is beyond childbearing age.

The biggest problem with a difference in age is a difference in maturity level that usually falls in line with age. Since most people's maturity will eventually plateau at a certain point (my best guess is usually the late twenties), once both of you have reached your respective maturity plateaus, age becomes much less of an issue. When you are less mature, it's sometimes harder to distinguish less important issues from more important ones, and it can be very frustrating if someone you are in a relationship with thinks that big issues aren't big, no matter how mature you are. If you can't tell that the issue is not big, it doesn't change the reality of the other person's feelings. Unlike having two bad communicators, if you are both incorrectly identifying small problems as bigger problems due to immaturity, at least you will have a chance to get on the same page about what to do about it because you will see the problem in the same way.

Race/Ethnicity – even though I vehemently believe that it should not be this way, either on principle or on logic, ethnicity is a much more difficult demographic to navigate than age, or any other demographic measurement for that matter. There is nothing in the New Testament that gives any prohibitions about two people of different races or ethnicities engaged in an exclusive romantic relationship. Sociologists have made entire careers on an issue that we're only going to spend a few paragraphs on. With that said, I am not attempting to be comprehensive here, but this topic does deserve a more comprehensive treatment.

If your family or friends view the person you are with as different than you or themselves (for any reason, but specifically if the differences are stemmed by perceived or real differences in ethnicity or culture), this will have the potential to create problems. I hope we will someday get to the point where the color of someone's skin truly has no bearing on that person's receptivity, and I recognize we are much, much further along to that end than we were even one generation ago, but we are not there yet. Much of the time, being of different ethnicities means you have come from different cultures and concerning the way the two of you relate with each other, cultural differences will likely be a major source of conflict. Different cultures teach different sets of expectations of its participants, their roles in pursuit and marriage, family, community involvement, perspectives on education, finances, entertainment, and so many other things. Pursuit between cultures can create challenges that will not exist within a single culture, but on the other hand, will give you a unique opportunity to appreciate and understand aspects of God's character that you would not otherwise.

Religious denomination – if you followed step one, this will likely not be a big deal for you. For better or worse, church communities do a consistently good job of filtering out theological traditions and beliefs that vary from their own. If your church community is like most church communities and you follow step one before you get to step two, any theological differences you have will most likely be minor. If your Christian community does extend beyond one tradition, here are some things you want to be on the lookout for as you are looking. What are your thoughts on infant baptism or different types of discipline for children? What do you think about speaking in tongues? What does it mean to be baptized in the Holy Spirit and what are its implications? What is the role of the Church in personal salvation? What is the purpose and function of the sacraments? If you answer some of these questions differently than the other person, for some traditions, it can be enough of a disconnect for you to not consider entering into a romantic relationship with that person. The really good news is that since you are finding out all of these things in the course of a normal friendship, without getting attached in a dating relationship, you can have robust disagreements on the dividing issue with your friend of the opposite sex for years to come without having to make any really hard choices, break any hearts, or cause any emotional scarring. Men and women can be friends, and so can

Christians who come from different traditions and have different understandings of theology.

Interests – One last thing. It matters very little if you have hobbies in common. Some people say you both will want to be active in the same types of ways or sedentary in the same types of ways, but if you exhibit all the characteristics from earlier, this will not matter very much at all. Now that you know who to look for and, more importantly, who you will want to be when you start looking, it's time to make sure you're on the same page about getting married. Next, we learn how to move from being simply friends in community to two people who are getting married.

The Intentional Pursuit

When you recognize that she has, in fact, struck your fancy and you want to proceed, go back to your wise counsel and tell them who she is and that you are considering a pursuit. If they have no objections, you are ready to start. As you are praying about it, consider her high-quality character as a confirmation. I have a feeling I will need to say this several times for it to sink in: you are not praying about whether she likes you or whether she wants you to pursue her or whether she's interested in you or whether she is ready or anything of the sort on her behalf. All those things do matter, men, but none of those things matter an ounce for you in this part of the process. You do not need to consider them, and you absolutely do not need to wait for a confirmation from God about any of these things or anything like them. Many, many guys can get trapped in fear or uncertainty and don't move forward at this point in the old paradigm; but remember: you're not in the old paradigm.

First of all, if you are friends already like I've implored you to be, then you are already comfortable talking to her. You don't have to get nervous engaging her in conversation. If you have developed community like I have suggested, you've already potentially spent time with her and other girls, so you won't be uncomfortable talking to her simply because she's a girl you like. If you're lucky, there are lots of people who see the virtue of this paradigm and it's natural for a guy to ask one girl to get coffee or something else so there will be nothing out of the ordinary about your interactions. If everyone in your community has bought into this, the unnecessary pressure of anticipation in guys giving girls attention goes away. And as I will explain in just a little bit, the unnecessary apprehension of a female towards a guy she doesn't want to like her, but likes her anyway, will also not be there.

There are a couple of goals you are trying to achieve by proceeding this way. Avoid the false commitment of relationship statuses. You're not going to be a couple who is not admitting that you're a couple. You are also intentionally avoiding romance or anything with sexual undertones. Romantic thoughts cloud judgment and run contrary to logical thoughts. At this point in your decision-making, you need to rely more on rational thinking than romantic thoughts or sexual impulses. You are intentionally avoiding opportunities to think or act like a commitment exists when you know the danger of false commitment and the fact that any "commitment" short of engagement is fraudulent.

The most obvious point (although not the most important point) of proceeding in this way is you will be much more likely to maintain sexual purity in your relationship. Sexual purity is probably not a problem in any other relationship you have with anyone else. Stewarding this relationship in a way that runs contrary to the way the world says will make this relationship just as likely to easily avoid sexual impurity or compromise as with every other friendship you have.

Proceeding in pursuit without initiating a traditional dating relationship will encourage you to continue your involvement in healthy community. The focus of your interactions will be with community in mind more than the person in whom you have interest. Instead of finding yourself in a relationship where you have to make a point to spend some time with others, as the two of you grow closer, you will focus on developing a healthy relationship in community. Keep in mind, once you get married, you will both want and need to be in a broader community, but it's not always the most natural thing to do, especially for those couples who tended to isolate themselves while they were dating. This method will set your marriage up to exist in, benefit from, and add to a healthy church community.

But how do I, as a guy, start this intentional non-dating relationship with one particular female that is different than all my other non-dating relationships with females?

Simple. You talk to her and you tell her your intentions. At no point should a man's intentions be a mystery to a female in whom he has a specific interest. Say something like this:

I've seen several things I like about your character and I would like to be more intentional about getting to know you. I'm not asking for you to assess whether you have an interest in me any more than the friendship we already have. I want you to be aware I am going to want to try and spend more time with you. I only ask that you begin prayerfully assessing my character as well. If I ever ask to spend time with you and you don't want to for whatever reason, please don't feel any pressure or obligation to say yes when I ask. My interest in you is not contingent on reciprocal interest from you.

But don't be awkward about it.

One of the beauties of this method is that it implicitly forces good communication between the two of you and it exposes bad communication between the two of you. When you, as a man, declare your intentions at first, you are creating a specific accountability to her and everyone as to your behavior. If it ever becomes clear to you that you do not want to walk on a path that will lead to marriage, you make it clear by telling her. The beauty is, though, that even in telling her, you don't have to change the way you act towards her because you have only been behaving like a friend this entire time. If it ever becomes clear to the woman that she will not want to eventually be married to you for whatever reason, she makes it clear to you by telling you. The beauty is, though, you don't have to be concerned about losing a friend based on your decision because you are not saddled with regret or heartache or wanting to avoid the other person.

What if I cannot ever see myself being married to him?

Ladies, if you realize at some point that you cannot ever see yourself being married to him specifically, this is what you say: *I realized that I cannot ever see myself being married to you.* Don't blame God. Don't blame a current circumstance in your life. Don't accidentally give false hope by trying to be euphemistic or by putting time conditions in your explanation. Ladies, don't say, *"Right now,* I can't see us together." If you can't see it right now, but you are not sure, wait until you're sure to say anything. In fact, the only time when you need to be able to see yourself together definitively is when he proposes marriage. You don't need to be able to imagine it at the first conversation, or the second conversation, or the thirty-second conversation. Give yourself an honest chance to evaluate him by not deciding either yes or no too quickly. At first, don't decide no to him too quickly. And when the time comes, don't decide yes to him too quickly. And I wish it didn't need to be said, but this conversation happens face to face, with zero exceptions.

So, what happens if he likes you and you don't like him back? Well first of all, if you are following along with me, then you were friends to begin with; so when you are talking about liking him, if you mean romantically, it's fine that you don't like him. If this is the case, this is what you get to look forward to as he proceeds. He's going to want to get to know you better, and you can do the same. You can still spend time with other guys if you like, and in fact, you can spend time one-on-one with other guys, though even now groups will be better most of the time. All the pressure is on him. You never have to say yes to spending time with him, but you can say yes without fear of misleading him or leading him on. Because you aren't leading at all. He decided to express a deeper interest in you without being prompted by you. He asked you for the chance to get to know you better. He is pursuing you. If his persistence is making you uncomfortable, tell him. Clearly. Say something like this: *The way you write a sonnet for me and hand-deliver it to my dorm room every morning makes me uncomfortable.* He is your friend, so you can tell him. You can be honest with a friend. Also, do the honorable thing by telling him before you complain to your friends about him. Take advantage of your friendship and tell him.

Ladies, you need to know that it is okay to spend intentional time with a male friend even if you are not physically attracted to him. If he is truly a friend, treat him like a friend. Think of him as a friend. Spend time with him as you would a friend. If he has read this book, he should be treating you like a friend as well, just like he was treating you before. Ladies, the first time you will ever have to commit to him anything is if he asks for your hand in marriage. In the meantime, enjoy your freedom and enjoy your friendship.

Ladies, whether you right now in this moment want him to express exclusive interest in you or not, you need to still expect that he is going to look for opportunities to spend time with you and other people in your interactions as well. Remember, it's sometimes much easier to evaluate a person in their interactions with other people around who are interacting with both of you. Also, you want to be comfortable interacting together with other people because if you end up getting married, you will be doing this a lot together.

A lot of times in society today, men will only move forward if there is no risk. A guy will be unlikely to ask a girl on a date if he doesn't think he has a chance of her saying yes. He isn't going to ask her to be his girlfriend unless he can tell that she is interested in him. Women pick up on this and in order to help these often-times clueless guys, a girl will feel compelled to expose her emotions first. She will feel compelled to become vulnerable first so that he will do the same. Female-first vulnerability needs to stop. Giving her reason to flirt with you to entice you to pursue her needs to stop.

Men, here is the idea in this part of this process. Up until now, your primary social intention has been to develop relationships with your Christian community. You have been intentionally getting to know (and getting to be known by) other guys your age, men who are older than you, older married couples, younger married couples, girls your age who you might never consider marrying, and girls your age who you might consider marrying someday. You have been intentionally not over-developing a friendship or a relationship with any lady (or ladies) with an eye towards exclusivity. Until now.

Now you shift your intentions. This shift of intentions is a deliberate thing you choose. It's not something you fall into. Now is not the time to wait until you are sure she is interested, and it will be an emotionally safe play for you to go after her. Never mask your intentions while your actions are demonstrating a specific interest in her. There are some guys who do this thing called "backdoor dating." If you spend enough time with someone in the right ways and talk about the right things, before you know it, people will think the two of you are dating. When enough people think the two of you are dating, sometimes that is enough outside pressure to cause a relationship to form. This tactic, whether it is done intentionally or not, is generally torturous on the female in the relationship, even if she does like the attention she's getting. It also usually leads to very avoidable and unnecessary confusion. Let's avoid anything at all that remotely resembles backdoor dating. This is why you let her know your intentions upfront.

Our society puts the burden of vulnerability way too much on the woman. This needs to change. The man needs to carry the lion's share of vulnerability. The man needs to be the one to initiate conversations about relationship status. The man needs to, at every point, be the one to express his emotions first. This is a very scary position for a man to find himself in. Have you ever told someone you like them, and you had no clue whether or not that person will reciprocate? It's a very scary place to be, but it is an incredibly flattering and honoring gesture for a man to do this to a female friend.

When a man does this for a woman (and, yes, it's for her not to her), he is demonstrating to her that he is taking her seriously – that she is worth being taken seriously. He is demonstrating an ability to make a decision, which is an ability all women want in a spouse. He is demonstrating the fact that he is brave. And men, make no mistake about it: when you communicate interest to a girl without any indication from her that she wants you to, or that she will be receptive to your declared interest, this is an uncomfortable thing. It will require a lot of courage from you. You can be courageous, or you can be comfortable, but you cannot be both. Hopefully, if you are a Spirit-indwelt follower of Christ, you are accustomed to doing things that require courage and are uncomfortable, so this won't be a first.

Practically, the amount of time you spend with her might not change at all, but the way you spend that time may change. Practically, you are still going to be organizing group events for lots of people, including her, to participate in, but now you are going to look for opportunities to interact with her more individually. You may increase your one-on-one outings as well, but not to the point where these are the majority of your interactions. If you limit your one-on-ones, it will be harder to accidentally slip into the world's dating pattern which you want to avoid. Please don't forget that even though the conventional dating model is less helpful, less healthy, and worth avoiding, it is still an attractive option because it is easier and because it is common. Hopefully, if you are a Spirit-indwelt follower of Christ, you are accustomed to doing things that aren't easy or common.

In this arena the easy thing and the common thing are not your friends. Being brave and assertive as a man is not easy or common, but it is better for your relationships. Being clear and honest in communication as a man is not easy or common, but it is better for your relationships. Being emotionally vulnerable first as a man is not easy or common, but it is better for your relationships. And for you ladies, waiting patiently is not easy (though a little more common), but it is better for your relationships. You don't want easy. You don't want common. You want to be wise and make choices that will look different than the rest of the world but will benefit you all along the way – and end up benefiting the person you marry in ways you can't even imagine in the future.

So, what if a guy has a conversation with me about looking towards marriage and I'm not ready? If you know that you're not in a place in your life where you are ready to begin a serious relationship, you need to let him know that. It's never too soon to tell him if you think you're not ready. Whether you like the guy or not, if you realize you're not ready to walk down the road to marriage, tell him. You can still be friends, but it is not honoring to him to have him alone on a road towards marriage if he thinks you're on the same road but you're not. If you simply want his attention without regard for his intentions, that is selfish.

You need to know if you're not in a place where you should be realistically looking for a spouse. Are you in high school? Are you a college freshman? Are you writing a dissertation that will command almost all your social time? If you know your life will not, for any number of reasons, allow you to get married in the foreseeable future, you need to be honest with the young man who has taken the brave step of declaring his interest. Keep in mind that you letting him know does not cut him out of your life because he is not being friends only with the possibility of something more; he's your friend because he's your friend. He just wanted to explore the possibility of something more because he thinks you're awesome.

Men, if she doesn't know about this new paradigm but you do, you get to initiate the conversation and explain your intentions. This is best. You need to be driving all the relationship conversations anyway, so you get to explain without being taken off guard, and because you are the man, following this method is entirely up to you.

Ladies, if he doesn't know about this new paradigm, at the point you begin to sense he is moving towards commitment, you can explain it then. Give him a copy of this book if it will help. If you feel uncomfortable talking about this with him, you're probably not really in a place where you should be committing with him to any extent anyway. If he does not receive your wishes well, or at least try to better understand where you're coming from, that temperament is probably a good indication he's got some growing to do before he is ready.

When you do start spending one-on-one time together, it will still be as friends. There aren't going to be any goodnight kisses. There aren't going to be any late-night movies where you hold hands under a blanket. There aren't going to be any sensual sunscreen back rubs. There aren't going to be any physical acts that fall on the spectrum of sexuality. Even though you are starting to take steps towards being married (namely finding the person), you are still not yet married, so you may not begin acting like you are.

Men, you are going to start paying closer attention to things about her character than you already have. If you haven't already, you are going to start finding out about her future career and family aspirations.

Ladies, if you stop having fun spending time with him, or if you, for any reason, want to stop spending time with him, let him know. One more crucial thing for you, ladies: you need to give him the freedom to ask to spend time with you as much as he wants to, but you must feel the freedom to say no any and every time he asks if you feel so inclined.

Men are probably realizing that there is an inequity in the relationship at this point. Men, when you make your intentions known upfront, you have declared and decided that you are exclusively directing your interest to this one female. Men, pursue only one woman at a time. She, however, has not and will not commit exclusively to you until you get on one knee and propose marriage. This also means that if there are other guys in your friend circle who might have been interested in this same lady, they might, as the Lord leads them and as buffeted by older wise counsel, declare the same thing you just did to the same girl. And she has the freedom to say yes to their invitations as much as she has the freedom to say yes to yours.

There will never come a point where the woman should feel obligated to say yes to the man. She should say yes because she wants to say yes. You should not see her saying yes to other men as a negative sign if she still says yes to you.

Men, if she says no a couple of times to invitations, you don't have to take it as a sign that she wants you to stop giving her more attention, but if it turns into a pattern, you can ask. Don't forget, you are friends first and hopefully if you have reached the point where you would choose this one girl, you have also reached the point where you can ask her if her "no" is to the request or if her "no" is to you. And just to be clear, if she makes it clear[102] to you that she does not want you to pursue her, do not pursue her.

Ladies, if you are convinced that this method is the best way to move towards marriage and he disagrees with your strategy, give him a copy of this book. Seriously. Tell him to demonstrate his desire for a commitment by chasing you until he's ready to marry you. If he's young and immature enough, he will get tired of chasing you, which will be great for you because if he's not in it for the long haul, you just saved yourself loads of wasted emotion and heartache. If he gets frightened at the prospect of ending up with you forever instead of simply as a girlfriend, this is very good because you don't want him wasting your time or monopolizing your attention and affections when there are other guys who are actually serious about being with you. Heistand and Thomas say, "In our public teaching on this topic we frequently tell women 'Don't give your heart away until you know what he plans to do with it.' And we tell the men, 'Stop being irresponsible. Don't try to win a woman's heart unless you plan on keeping it.'"[103]

It is irresponsible for a woman to give her heart away to a man who has not pledged to keep it and it is negligent for a man to try

---

102 Being clear means using direct, unequivocal words.

103 *Sex, Dating, and Relationships: A Fresh Approach*, Hiestand, G., Thomas, J. Crossway 2012 page 63

to win the heart of a lady if he does not plan on keeping it. Ladies, if he is not playing for keeps, then he is just playing around. Don't let anyone play around with your heart.

By the way, if this situation happens where multiple guys express their intentions to one girl, each of you needs to keep in mind, you are not trying to win a competition. The difference between competing for a girl and against another guy is this: your actions and pursuit aren't influenced by what the other guy is or isn't doing. Also, if you are in the same friend circle, you will still be organizing group activities and events that the other guy is still invited to attend. Ladies, if for some reason there are two or more guys vying for your attention and tension or turmoil does arise between them, it is not your fault nor is it your responsibility to help resolve it. If anyone asks you to get involved in any type of mediation or resolution, you need to stay out of it.

Men, if at any point it becomes clear for any reason that you are no longer interested in pursuing a deeper relationship with her, step one: pray about it; step two: talk to those older, wiser adults in your life about it. Tell them what you're thinking and why before you tell her. You are going to want to be able to clearly articulate your reasons to them, because when you tell her, the honorable thing would be to clearly articulate your reasons to her. This decision has the same emotional weight of a breakup, even if it lacks the brunt of the sting. If you decide to stop an intentional pursuit, it will be disappointing and it will be painful, but the pain and disappointment will not be compounded by all of the time you wasted with this one person (because you've still been spending lots of time with other people too), or the physicality you wish you could take back (because you clearly have not been sexually physical with someone else in a neighbor relationship category), or the private, intimate things you've shared but wish you hadn't (because all the things you talked about with this person, you would have shared with many of the friends you have gotten to know well), or the fact that a part of your life is now missing (because you never started to orient your life around this person in this first place; they never were your last call of the day, or the main person you text during the day when something silly or funny happened). It will be disappointing, but you get to share that disappointment with a large number of people who are older than you and younger than you and your same age because you developed community and you will have that many more people praying for you. It will be disappointing, but you don't have to worry about never talking to him or her again. The disappointment will not be compounded by regret or guilt or shame.

A couple of thoughts about ending a pursuit. Depending on how long the intentional pursuit lasted, you might need to take time and give the other person space, but you need to communicate this to your friend. If you committed to doing something with him or her (*e.g.* going to a Greek formal, or a Christmas party), as the male, ask the female if she still wants you to go with her if it's her event. If the event is yours, DO NOT break off the event with her unless she wants to, but do ask if she will still go with you. Also, be careful how you ask if she still wants to go. Say something like, "I would still really like for you to come to my family's beach house for the Fourth of July if you want to, but completely understand if you don't. You don't need to decide now, but please let me know when you are ready."

Abstaining from displays of romantic affection will especially make the process of ending pursuit much less painful. Heistand and Thomas say in *Sex, Dating and Relationships: A Fresh Approach*,

> There is nothing a person can discover in a dating relationship or courtship that cannot equally be discovered through a dating friendship. Life dreams, priorities, values, backgrounds, and character qualities can all be gleaned

through a friendship. One does not need to establish a separate category of relationship to discern these things. In fact, we would argue that these important character qualities and life goals can be even more readily discerned within the context of a dating friendship. Many dating relationships are based solely upon the romantic and sexual attraction that exists between the couple. But strip that away and they will discover that they have almost nothing in common and really nothing to talk about.[104]

Romance and sexuality will almost necessarily cloud your ability to think clearly about the other person. When you become infatuated with someone, it becomes very difficult to be discerning and see that person clearly. It is so important that you do pay attention to character, emotional stability, and the way he or she exists in community. It is not helpful or wise to allow romantic displays of affection to cloud your assessment of the person.

Part of the advantage of withholding romantic affection is it will motivate the man to not dawdle. Men these days can have the luxury of dawdling with commitment because you get certain benefits of marriage without the responsibilities that go along with them.

So what kinds of things do you do while you are seeking clarity? Spend your time wisely. Figure out what things she enjoys doing and do them together. Find things that the two of you like to do together and have fun! Figure out in what ways she enjoys serving in the community and serve with her if you can (if she works at a battered woman's shelter, you might not be able to help in the same way she does, but maybe you can pull weeds in the

104 *Sex, Dating, and Relationships: A Fresh Approach*, Hiestand, G., Thomas, J. Crossway 2012 page 99

garden or mow the lawn or help in the kitchen while she is serving). Just like with your other friends, find activities and events where you can talk with and interact with one another. Get coffee with her and a friend. Please don't forget that you're not foregoing community. Also keep in mind that you will want to find out things about her like what her career priorities are, whether she wants a big or small family, if she is a spender or a saver, but you can still go to coffee with her and one or two other people and find out the same information from the other people as well, which will help with the health of your community of friends. Most of the helpful information you will want to find out about him or her can be found out in conversations that are more than one-on-one.

What about meeting my family? I live in a different city five states away. How can I take him home to meet Mom and Dad without a commitment? How do I introduce her at the family reunion without having my entire extended family read this book to understand what we're doing? Well first of all, extend an invitation to meet your family when it's time. Ladies, as the first thing he did was declare his interest, you should not at all be surprised when he asks you to meet his parents at some point. Also, you should feel the freedom to invite him to meet your family when you feel comfortable. Don't feel obligated to reciprocate an invitation to meet a family, even after you have accepted his invitation; but if it's time, then it's time. By the way, if you don't know if it's time or not, ask the wise older people who have been walking with you through this entire process. "Without counsel plans fail, but with many advisers they succeed."[105]

Men, once your clarity about this woman leads you to the decision that you want her to be your wife, now it is the time to act! It now becomes your job to win her affections and win her heart. Now, after you have decided that you want to propose marriage,

---

105 Proverbs 15:22

you can begin walking down the path to romance. This, by the way, is the bridge to the marriage relationship. First, the man must decide after having done all his homework, that he wants her heart until death parts them. He has to decide to want to be in the marriage relationship and everything that comes with it. Once he has made this decision, it is finally time to stir and awaken love. When a man has decided on one woman to be his wife and nothing short of that commitment threshold, he can begin to initiate romance.

However, even as romance is initiated the sexual purity standard still cannot be compromised, and this still means no sexual immorality, no lusting, or previewing any sexuality that is meant for marriage. But you can gently begin increasing the three T's.[106] You can begin looking to spend more one-on-one time with her (still be wise about it; not in your apartment alone, not late at night, not in times and places where you are baiting yourself to compromise sexually). Carefully change the way you talk to her. Start telling her how beautiful she looks. Start being more overt about verbally expressing your feelings towards her (you are probably going to want to hold onto the "L" word for as long as you are able and bring it out at the right time, but at this point it's entirely up to you). If you're a poetry guy, try some of that. If you bake, buy a heart-shaped cookie cutter and have at it. You are trying to win her heart, so use all your resources and sweep her off her feet.

The third T, touch, comes into play as well, but you really need to be extra careful about this one. You might want to grab her hand as you are walking down the sidewalk. You might want to give a gentle squeeze on the arm when the two of you share an inside joke in the middle of a crowd. You will want to be very, very careful about kissing, even in a non-sexual manner. This is the hardest balance to find in the pursuit, but I highly recommend erring on the side of less touch. Purity before marriage paves the

---

106 Time, talk, touch – as described in the last chapter

way to intimacy within marriage. As you have gotten to the point that you want to marry her without any degree of sensual touch, she can get to the same place without that type of touch as well.

Another thing you are going to want to do at this point is buy a ring. It will be easier for her to tell that you're serious when you ask her to marry you if you have a ring to give her. Plus, there is no gesture more romantic than getting on one knee and asking for a girl's hand in marriage. After you buy the ring, but before you give it to her and ask her to marry you, is a good time to talk to the girl's father about marrying his daughter.

Ladies, if you're following along with this new paradigm, a male friend has expressed interest in getting to know you better with the idea that you might be someone he could marry someday. He has asked you to give him the chance to get to know you and asked that you would do the same. You haven't increased your affection towards him like you might someone who was trying to be your boyfriend, but you have grown in fondness towards him like anyone would as they get to know a friend and spend more time with that friend. As you have gotten to know him, you have grown to like him even more. He may even be growing to be one of your best friends; but he's not your only friend or even your first friend because you are still very deliberate about spending time in community with both girls and guys, people your age, and older people in different stations in life. Because you are balanced, you have not accidentally grown emotionally dependent on him. You recognize your similarities and differences and you like being around him because of those similarities and those differences, but you are in no way beholden to him.

You might be attracted but you're not unduly attached. The course of your friendship has not allowed for undue attachment. You are clearly friends without romance. You aren't physically compromised, emotionally compromised, or spiritually conflicted.

You see him for who he is, really. And you are comfortable being your real self around him. There is no more pressure or obligation to spend time with him than any of your other friends, but hopefully, eventually you recognize there might be more of a desire to spend time with him (which is why you've been intentional about maintaining those other relationships).

Then one day your friend asks you to marry him. Maybe you sensed it coming and maybe you didn't realize he felt this way right now. Early on, maybe even a year or so ago, when he told you his intentions to get to know you with marriage in mind, he asked you to let him know if you ever realized that you would definitely not see yourself getting married to him. You haven't done this because you honestly could see yourself getting married to him, and now he is asking you to be his wife.

A few weeks ago, this friend started acting like he was smitten by you. He began doing things that seemed to be intentionally drawing at your affections. This entire time he has been intentional. He has been intentional in the way he began getting to know you, the conversations, the activities, the opportunities for the two of you to serve together, the times spent with you and with other people, and eventually the way he began to deliberately try to win your heart because he decided definitively that yours is the only heart he wants, forever. And now he asks you, and you get to decide.

You may have already decided that he is the one you want. Your heart might have been primed and ready for months now, so as soon as he sought your affections, they were there for the taking. Maybe you had been enjoying the friendship, but you weren't convinced that you wanted to give your heart to him, so now as he is asking you this question of questions, you have a decision to make.

But this is one of the beauties of this method. He has to ask without really knowing. I mean, he kind of knows. His romantic gestures were well received by you. Otherwise, you would have told him so like you would to any well-meaning friend who is acting in a way towards you that you don't fully embrace. But since from the beginning he told you where this might be heading, you don't have to guess at and possibly misinterpret his intentions. You also don't have to try and coax these feelings out of him before he is ready. You don't have to be the vulnerable one who tosses your feelings out like bait in order to lure him and reel him in. This was the road he asked you to walk down, so perhaps the hard part for you was adjusting to his pace. When he finally asks, you don't have to feel the pressure of a friendship ending if you say no. You don't have to feel the societal obligation to say yes because you didn't break it off before the relationship got to this point. You get to say yes because the two of you have arrived at this place and it's the very place you want to be and the person you want to be with.

Step Four: Right to the Wedding

WHAT WE HAVE done is changed the order of things. This entire time, you haven't been ignoring attraction. You have been bridling romantic affection. You have been developing true chemistry absent of sexuality. Sexuality is enough to hold any relationship together for a while, but if sexuality is the basis of your relationship, any bond forged by it will fade and probably falter or fail. But when your connection and chemistry is based on a pure friendship demonstrated by Christ-like character, sexual intimacy will make your bond inseparable.

Society tells us to use sexuality to build the bonds of relationships. Before you have truly gotten to know the person, you might be in a relationship that is predicated on physical affection. And it takes a while to be able to truly get to know someone even if the other person doesn't have a facade, trying to be the person they think will be more likely to win your attention and affection. The more sexuality you express, the more difficult it is to truly discern the other person's character. The more sexuality you express, the more difficult it is to break the connection you forged, no matter how little time has passed. Society has it all backwards and if we buy into it, we are all setting ourselves up for relational failure and the worst kind of heartache. We don't have to do this.

When we act like the dating relationship has different rules of engagement[107] than any other unique relationship that is not family or marriage, we are doing ourselves a great disservice. If we don't allow our culture's rules of sexuality to engulf us, clouding the way we interact with the opposite sex, we will be able to see the people around us much more clearly, and also be able to identify much more quickly who has the traits we want to end up with when it comes time for the altar.

Even if you have read this book, there will be times where you will want to skip the process. You will want to latch on to one person, especially if he or she seems great and seems like he or she is interested in you. Everyone likes being liked. Everyone. You will want to ignore or expedite the process, even if you agree with it. Don't do this. Trust the process.

If the person you're interested in skipping the process for is actually the one you're looking for, if he or she seems worthy enough to skip the process, he or she will still be there months later when the time comes if you don't skip; and by the way, if he or she isn't there, that simple fact is one piece of evidence that supports the idea that this one was not the best one for you.

When it comes to getting married, please don't rush. It is possible to go too slowly, but it is much easier to move too fast. Until you decide. Once you decide, move as quickly to marriage as humanly possible. Give yourself enough time to plan the wedding of your dreams, but no more than that. The point of engagement isn't to do more vetting of the person you're going to marry. You don't ask until you have purposed in your heart that she is the one God has for you. You do not say yes unless you are certain that he has first proven himself worthy by both his character and his

---

107 No pun intended.

pursuit, and you have determined that your heart will be safe with him in a committed marriage relationship.

The way the world is telling you to date does work, but it does not work very well. If you're looking for drama and conflict in your romantic exploits, the world is very good at that. If you are looking for a path that is physically, emotionally, spiritually, and relationally dangerous, listen to the lessons of the world. The world loves to bait people to the edge of the moral cliff and then casts shame and mockery on the ones who fall over the edge. You don't have to walk near the edge of the cliff when you're walking down the path to romance. There is a way that not only steers clear of the cliff's edge, but is a shorter, more direct path to your end goal and you will grow healthier as you follow it. The way I'm suggesting can be thrilling and exciting; it's just not dangerous. The way that I am suggesting can be edifying, encouraging and fun. The way I'm suggesting works better.

What if the way you decide to go about dating could help you be a better husband or wife? Imagine if the way you pursue marriage intentionally helped you learn how to be a leader in your relationships. Imagine if you practiced being open, honest and vulnerable in ways that you won't have to unlearn as you get to know your spouse. Imagine not putting yourself through practice divorces before getting married so the very idea of a potentially temporary committed relationship is a contradiction in terms. Imagine if you and all the singles around you focused on becoming more like Jesus Christ in both word and deed; that a large, healthy community of Christ-followers were cheering for you, praying for you, doing whatever they could to help you as you move from one station in life to the next. Imagine if you were to get out of your own way as you're looking for someone and actually gave yourself your best chance to find someone who has the character qualities you would want to be with forever.

What if the very way you went about interacting in community helped you grow in love and joy and peace, patience, kindness, goodness, faithfulness, gentleness and self-control? What if you were inspiring everyone around you to do the same, whether they are married or not? What if the very way you went about caring for the people in your community was equipping you to be a better listener, a better empathizer, a more understanding person? What if the way you go about finding your spouse could better equip you to avoid unnecessary relational conflict once you are married; or more importantly, help you traverse even the unavoidable relationship conflict that will inevitably find you in your marriage? The way you find your spouse will help prepare you to be a better spouse and have a God-glorifying marriage.

Chances are if you are reading this and you are not yet married, you will be some day. I wrote this because I don't want your path to marriage to be any more difficult than it has to be. I wrote this because you have the potential to avoid so many unnecessary emotional scars and bruises as you are trying to find the person for you. I wrote this so that you don't accidentally and unnecessarily waste your time trying to find the person you would be best with by using a dating process that makes finding that person so much more difficult. I wrote this because finding a spouse can be a pleasant experience. I wrote this because I believe that if we start with the Bible as the very foundation of how to interact in our relationships, the likelihood of us walking in a matter worthy of the Lord will drastically increase. Marriage is a wonderful gift from God. We can find joy in the journey from singleness to marriage by honoring God every step of the way. Finally, my dear reader, trust in the Lord with all your heart, and lean not on your own understanding. In all your ways, acknowledge Him, and He shall direct your paths.

Acknowledgements

I want to thank Christopher Wesley Cook for trusting me to give a different kind of relationship talk that one time at Refuge leadership. I owe a debt to everyone to whom I gave early copies of this: Hannah Beckett Akuiyibo, Chase Baldwin, John Don, Hans Googer, Charles Hedman, Patrick Hulehan, Erica Rhodes, Caleb Smith (the audio version). Thanks to Cameron and Tricia Smith who parsed my words, sharpened my articulations, and constantly pointed me back to the gospel. Thanks to Mike Meyers, Michael Rhodes, Rachel Street, and Jordan Wilson for the artistic advice. Thanks to George and Bettejean Cramer for giving me an inside look at a fabulous marriage. Thanks to Steve Fox for challenging and honing my thoughts. Thanks to Jenny Thompson for doing me the small favor of preserving my sanity. Catherine Barrack, you helped to make every single aspect of this book better. Thank you.

Thanks to Katherine Webb who trusted me and gave me an inside glimpse into her heart as she searched for the love her life. Thanks to Jennifer and Martina for being my inspiration. Thanks to Paul Gravois and Hannah McLain, who are probably in this book a lot more than anyone else. Thanks to Britteny Adams for challenging the way I thought about romance and its place in a healthy relationship. Thanks to Levie Chustz for teaching me how to love people. Thanks to Mrs. Laurie Godshall for meeting with me every day after school in 10th grade until I wasn't the worst at grammar. Thanks to Laura Gordey for telling me that I'm a good writer. Thanks to Bill Cassidy for having a conversation with me about my goals and challenging me to realize that I wanted to write a book as well.

And to mom and dad.

Index

E

exclusivity 50, 54, 56, 57, 61, 62, 63, 64, 67, 68, 71, 76, 94, 95, 102, 103, 117, 118, 144, 145, 151, 152, 156
    ownership 63, 64, 65, 66, 67
    territorialism 57

F

flirting 80, 81, 82, 83, 84, 85, 86, 87, 88, 116, 119, 152

G

gospel 17, 19, 20, 21, 22, 23, 76, 170

J

jealousy 50
Jesus 13, 14, 15, 16, 19, 21, 26, 27, 28, 39, 40, 47, 53, 70, 98, 102, 111, 130, 131, 137, 139, 168

P

propitiation 25
pursuit 49, 50, 51, 57, 58, 85, 97, 102, 111, 119, 135, 137, 146, 147, 149, 151, 152, 156, 157, 158, 159, 162, 168

R

referenced works
    Brown Brené, The Power of Vulnerability, TEDx 52
    Dean, Ruthie and Michael, Real Men Don't Text 91
    Fox, Steven 13
    Fry, Hannah, The Mathematics of Love 143
    Gladwell, Malcolm, Blink: The Power of Thinking Without Thinking 59, 60
    Heistand and Thomas, Sex, Dating and Relationships: A Fresh Approach 79, 95, 157, 159, 169
    Herd, Jared, BigStuf Camps 37
    Kemp, Thomas, Refuge College Ministry 25
    Parker, Uncle Ben 115
    Simpson, P. Carnegie, The Fact of Christ 24
    Simpson, Stephen, What Women Wish You Knew About Dating 90, 92
    Stanley, Andy, The New Rules of Love, Sex and Dating 41
    Stott, John, The Cross of Christ 25
    The Late, Late Show with James Corden 9
romance 31, 74, 84, 85, 139, 148, 160, 162, 168, 170

CPSIA information can be obtained
at www.ICGtesting.com
Printed in the USA
LVHW092303150219
607775LV00001B/49/P